How to Say It®
to Your Cat

How to Say It®
to Your Cat

Solving Behavior Problems

in Ways Your Cat Will Understand

JANINE ADAMS

Prentice Hall

The health-related information in the book is not intended as medical advice. Its intent is informational and educational. Please consult a veterinarian should the need for one be indicated.

Prentice Hall Press
Published by The Berkley Publishing Group
A member of Penguin Group (USA) Inc.
375 Hudson Street
New York, New York 10014

Prentice Hall Press edition: November 2003

Library of Congress Cataloging-in-Publication Data

Adams, Janine.
    How to say it to your cat : solving bahavior problems in ways your cat will understand /
by Janine Adams.—1st Perigee ed.
        p. cm.
    Includes index.
    ISBN 0-7352-0329-6
    1. Cats—Behavior.   2. Cats—Training.   3. Human-animal communication.   I. Title.

SF446.5.A32 2003
636.8'0887—dc21

                                                            2003045959

Printed in the United States of America

This book is dedicated to Joe, my wonderful orange tabby, whose only fault is he doesn't display more problem behaviors for me to learn from. It's also dedicated to Flip, my cat-loving standard poodle, who helped us select Joe.

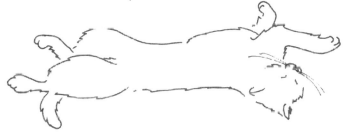

Contents

part one
General Care of Your Cat   1

part two
Keeping Your Cat Healthy   83

part three
Indoor-Outdoor Issues   141

part four
Solving Specific Behavior Challenges   163

Acknowledgments

I wish to thank my mother, Betty Adams, a true cat lover, who instilled in me in early childhood a love and appreciation for cats.

Thank you to Michael Snell, my agent, for bringing this project to me. And to Sheila Curry Oakes and Teresa Hennessy of Perigee Books, who are always pleasant and cheerful.

Thanks to certified TTouch practitioner Shannon Wilkinson, of Portland, Oregon, for valuable input on TTouch and for being such a great friend; to Sally Brown, for her wonderful illustrations and unflagging support; to Libby Mitchell, whose devotion to her animals is so inspiring and who is always willing to give me the benefit of her experience; and a special group of Internet friends: Gina Barnett, Ann Daugherty, Amy Heggie, and Susan Lennon, fabulous cat owners all, whose perspective on cats has been extremely valuable to me.

And, finally, a big thank-you to my husband, Barry Marcus, who supports me in everything I do.

Unraveling the Mysteries of Feline Communication

C ats are mysterious animals. Or at least many people think they are. They don't react to situations like people do. Nor do they react like dogs, probably the most familiar animal to humans. This makes people view cats as unpredictable. Yet if you understand the nature of cats and what makes them tick, they become much more predictable.

Once you learn about the origins of cats and how their wild ancestors (or counterparts) lived, new levels of understanding open up to you. And if you couple that knowledge with an understanding of how cats communicate, your cat will become much less of a mystery.

Origins

The domestic cat is much closer to its wildcat ancestors than the dog is to its wolf ancestors. Humans have done much less to manipulate the genetics of cats than they have with dogs. While there are variations in coat length and color and some differences in head and face shape among cat breeds, there is not the diversity in appearance that is seen in dogs. And the similarity in appearance between most domestic cats and wildcats is much closer than between most dogs and wolves. The vast majority of domestic cats are not pedigreed and are not of a specific breed. In the U.S. they're simply called domestic shorthairs or domestic longhairs.

But it's not just in appearance and lack of genetic manipulation that cats are similar to wildcats. While most housecats enjoy the company of their human (feline and canine) family members, like their wild counterparts, they are still much more solitary creatures than dogs or humans. In the wild they tend to live and hunt alone (though colonies of feral cats do live together around a shared food source).

This innate need for solitary hunting and the territoriality that surrounds it (to keep competitors away from the prey) mean that we must alter our expectations of cats. They're not small dogs, or furry people. They're beings hardwired to watch for prey, to kill and eat it, and to look out for competitors. Cats are small-enough creatures that they have to be concerned about becoming prey themselves. They're ever vigilant in watching for predators and making themselves invisible to them. That's why they are so fastidious with regard to cleanliness—they wash themselves after eating to rid themselves of the smell of food that might attract predators. They bury their urine and feces so it will escape the notice of predators. They eliminate far away from where they eat in order to keep predators away from their nest.

So how can such a being be happy inside a house? No prey, no predators, no hunting . . . what's a cat to do? You can help your cat stay happy and sane as a housecat by providing prey for him. I'm not suggesting you let live mice or birds loose in the house. But through interactive toys (the fishing-pole type) you can help your cat use his hunting skills and exercise that mental muscle. Indoor cats may not have predators, but as any cat owner who has moved suddenly toward her cat and watched him hurriedly skulk away knows, you can't always convince cats of that.

Cats who were brought up as kittens inside families can be very social with their human family members, but they may be less so with strangers. Even once-feral cats can be tamed and brought inside, though they're less likely to interact heavily with their humans. But even in the house, and even when they enjoy spending the evening on a human's lap, cat behavior is still governed by that hardwired need to hunt and not be hunted. Understanding that can help you understand their behavior.

How Your Cat Communicates

Cats use a variety of means to communicate with one another and with their human family members. Most of these, like vocalizations, body language, purring, and touch, are detectable by humans. But one special means of communication is ever present to cats, but undetectable by humans.

PHEROMONES

Cats use pheromones—chemicals produced by scent glands under their fur—to mark territory and communicate with other cats. If you understand the meaning behind using various types of pheromones, you can understand what your cat is saying.

The pheromone-laden scent glands can be found around the mouth, on the forehead, paw pads, and the anus. The pheromones that come from the cheeks and forehead have a calming effect on the cat. They're used to mark the nest (and the cat's people). The scent glands in the cat's anus produce pheromones that are released when he sprays urine. Cats produce these pheromones during anxiety or excitement. The cat also has scent glands in his paw pads. He deposits pheromones whenever he scratches, which helps him mark his territory (in addition to the visual marks that the scratches leave). Cats often scratch during periods of agitation or excitement.

When your cat rubs his head against something—including you—he's marking it with his facial pheromones. Experts feel that this is an emotionally stabilizing activity for the cat, since the absence of the cat's own scent is anxiety producing. Cats will also rub other cats in their family, and even dogs they're

	Friendly	Playful	Afraid
Eyes		Dilated pupils	Dilated pupils
Ears	Pointed slightly forward	Pricked forward	Flattened, pointing down and back
Whiskers	Pointed sideways or fanned out and pointed forward (when alert)	Fanned out, forward facing	Pulled back
Hair Coat	Smooth		Raised along back and tail
Body Posture		Stalking	Crouched, often facing sideways to object of fear
Tail	Vertical	Various	Lashing or tucked close to body
Other	Nose-to-nose touching, head butting, vocal murmur	Occasional chattering	Growling, hissing, or spitting

bonded with. The head butt that cats do with one another and with their people is a loving gesture. Offering your cat your head to butt or your face for him to touch with his mouth or cheeks is also a loving gesture that he's sure to appreciate.

Urine marking (spraying) is a way for a cat to communicate to other cats that they're about to enter his territory. It's also a reaction to stress and anxiety. Urine marking is most important to unneutered males. Most people don't appreciate this odoriferous activity, however. Whereas the facial and paw-pad marking doesn't leave a smell that's detectable to the human nose, cat urine—particularly that from intact males—certainly does. Neutering is the best way to curb this

Offensively Aggressive	Fearfully Aggressive	Submissive
Wide-open eyes, direct stare, constricted pupils	Dilated pupils	Dilated pupils, avoids direct eye contact
	Flattened, facing down and back	Ears held flat
Fanned out, facing forward	Pulled back along the face	
Standing up along shoulders and tail	Standing up on end	Smooth
Forward facing with hindquarters raised	Arched back (Halloween posture); facing opponent sideways	Crouched, head down
Down	Up and over the back or low to the ground or inverted-U position	Down, close to body
Snarling	Open mouth; hissing, growling, or spitting	May make a "silent meow"

problem, or prevent it from starting, though a certain number of neutered and spayed cats continue to spray.

Why does a cat spray (that is, back up to the object he wants to mark and squirt, tail aquiver) rather than squatting to urinate as usual? Like a dog lifting his leg, a spraying cat deposits the scent right at the nose level of the animals he's trying to communicate with, where it can't be missed. Spraying tends to take place on the perimeter of a cat's territory, whereas rubbing happens in the inner sanctum. Cats don't tend to spray where they've left facial pheromones, nor do they tend to scratch there.

BODY LANGUAGE

Cats don't have as broad a vocabulary as dogs when it comes to body language. Dogs are more social beings, whose instincts are to live in packs, where communication is essential. For the solitary cat, body language is less vital. But if you keep your eye on your cat's eyes, ears, tail, whiskers, hair coat, and posture, you can get a hint about what he's communicating. Before long, it will become second nature to you.

It is possible to generalize about the position of the various body parts your cat uses to communicate. These general descriptions, which are clearly presented in Pam Johnson-Bennett's excellent book, *Think Like a Cat: How to Raise a Well-Behaved Cat—Not a Sourpuss,* are summarized in the tables on the preceding pages.

It's interesting to note that cats have very different body language from dogs. In fact, a posture that means one thing to a dog (for whom an erect tail is a sign of aggression, for example) means the opposite to a cat, who holds his tail erect as a friendly gesture. A dog who rolls on his back is showing submission, whereas a fearful cat on his back may be readying all four paws for attack. These vocabulary differences may be one reason that cats and dogs often don't automatically hit it off. But they can certainly become companions—or even friends—with time.

VOCALIZATIONS

Some cats are more talkative than others. Some breeds, particularly the Orientals, are known for being chatterboxes. Anyone who pays attention to their cat's vocalizations knows that there are a variety of tones and meanings. Not only do cats meow, they chirp, they chatter, and they murmur. Within that classic meow, there's a wide range of tones, lengths, and meanings. Once you start paying attention, you can discern your cat's "I'm hungry" yowl from his "play with me" meow or his "I'm content" mew.

This is even a matter of scientific study. Researchers at Cornell University analyzed people's reactions to feline vocalizations and discovered that the meows perceived by humans as more urgent or demanding were longer, with energy in the lower frequencies (Mee-O-O-O-O-W!). Meows perceived as being more pleasant, or less demanding, tend to be shorter, with the energy spread evenly through the high and low frequencies, starting high and going low (MEE-ow).

But it doesn't take a scientific study to tell most cat owners that they know when their cat is asking for dinner.

PURRING

A cat's purr is one of the most comforting sounds he makes. The vibration of his body while he's purring feels exquisite to the touch. It's a feline-only phenomenon (with the exception of civets, small catlike creatures; and raccoons) and it's not entirely understood by scientists. How cats purr and why they purr are topics under scientific scrutiny.

What seems to be accepted as truth is that cats purr for reasons other than to indicate contentment. Certainly in most instances purring is a sign that a cat is happy. But cats also purr in stressful situations (like at the veterinarian's office) and they're known to purr when they're very ill or dying.

A research study is seeking to prove that cats may purr to heal. The Fauna Communications Research Institute, a nonprofit organization dedicated to the study of bioacoustics, hypothesizes that the reason that cats heal more quickly than dogs from broken bones and other orthopedic problems, as well as from tissue injury, is the healing power of the purr.

Fauna Communications researchers have identified that cats purr at some of the exact frequencies that have been found to be therapeutic in humans for bone growth and fracture healing, pain relief, swelling reduction, wound healing, muscle growth and repair, tendon repair, mobility of joints, and the relief of breathing difficulties. The researchers feel that it is possible that evolution has provided the felines of this world with a natural healing mechanism for bones and other organs. It's called purring. They are currently gathering data to test the purr-healing theory (using veterinary case records—no animals are harmed in the study).

TOUCH

It may sound a little odd, but your cat uses touch to communicate with you. Gentle pats to your face, with claws sheathed, are a gesture of affection. Kneading your lap is a sign of love and trust—it simulates the behavior your cat learned as a nursing kitten as he kneaded his mother to stimulate the flow of milk. Rubbing his forehead or cheeks against you gives you the compliment of marking you as his. When your cat curls up in your lap or lies on your chest, it can be sublime for both of you—a time when you feel mutually connected.

How You Can Communicate With Your Cat

Communicating with your cat is not difficult. Through body language, spoken words, play, training, and even telepathic communication, we communicate our love and respect for our cats. We help them know how we want them to behave. And when we listen to their efforts to communicate with us, we acknowledge that communication is a two-way street.

BODY LANGUAGE

You're speaking "cat" when you offer your cat a head butt or let him touch you on the mouth with his lips. You're communicating love when you stroke him as he wants to be stroked (which he'll tell you by positioning his body just so). Approaching your cat in a nonthreatening way, by moving slowly, never startling him, and not looming over him, is one way you can use body language to communicate.

YOUR VOICE

Speaking out loud to your cat can be very effective. Cats probably understand far more words than we give them credit for. And they certainly pick up on the natural intonations of our language. They can tell when words are spoken with love rather than anger. They can discern soft from harsh. And they often respond accordingly.

Some people might think it's silly to talk aloud to your cat—or a sign that you've gone over the bend, but it helps your cat become accustomed to your language. It keeps the two of you company, and it can be a very effective way to communicate a message.

YOUR EYES

You can communicate with your cat through your eyes. Just as people do, cats understand that the eyes are the windows into the soul. Soften your eyes and look at your cat with love. Slowly close and then open your eyes. Don't be surprised if your cat returns this slow, loving blink.

While it's best to use your eyes to communicate love, a harsh, hard stare can be a sign of disapproval that your cat can understand.

TELEPATHIC COMMUNICATION

One way your cat communicates with you—and you with him, whether you know it or not—is through telepathy. I know that sounds a little crazy, but I believe it to be true. When I was researching my book, *You Can Talk to Your Animals: Animal Communicators Tell You How* (Howell Book House, 2000), I spoke with eleven professional animal communicators—people who are paid to communicate telepathically with people's animals—and scores of their clients. Time and time again, I heard how using the services of animal communicators benefited people and animals.

The services of an animal communicator can be very helpful, especially when you're dealing with a tricky or urgent problem. But everybody has the ability to communicate telepathically. Cats speak to us telepathically all the time. We humans can communicate right back—and "hear" what our cats are telling us. Unfortunately, most of us have closed off that part of our mind and so we don't take advantage of this skill, which has so much potential for helping us connect with and build relationships with our pets.

Simply by visualizing positive outcomes and speaking silently to our cats, we are communicating with them in ways they understand. Talking out loud to them works, too. If your cat is particularly verbal (and if you talk with her a lot), she may understand the words you say to her. But behind every utterance is a telepathic message. And your cat is very likely to pick up that message. So you can easily harness the power of telepathic communication by simply talking aloud to your cat. It can't hurt—and it might very well be effective. (The other side of this is that we should be careful about what we say around our cats, who might pick up on more than we expect. A flippant comment about sending the cat to a shelter—said in jest by a spouse—might actually be disturbing to the cat!)

In addition to talking, silently or out loud, to your cat, you can take it a step further and learn to receive the telepathic messages that he is sending to you. See the appendix for titles of books that can help you rediscover this skill. It's a matter of simply quieting your mind, sending a message to your cat by thinking it, then opening up your quiet mind for a response. Then comes the hardest part: believing that the response you receive—I can promise you that something will go through your mind—is coming from the animal. If you can get over that hurdle of trust, you can take your relationship with your animal to a deeper level.

PLAY

Exercise is important for all beings. Those of us who have dogs know the importance of taking them on regular walks, trips to the park, or at least playing chase or fetch games in the backyard. This not only gives dogs the exercise that their bodies need, it keeps them from going nuts out of boredom.

Cats are no different. Their bodies and minds need exercising. But how can a loving cat owner provide that exercise? Most cat owners don't take their cats for walks (though training your cat to walk on a leash is certainly possible). The answer is very simple: play with your cat. When you play with your cat, you communicate respect for his needs and you tell him that you enjoy doing things with him.

Sure, you provide toys for your cat to play with. Little furry mice, maybe small balls to bat around. But you really need to provide interactive play— games that the two of you play together—that simulates hunting. Remember that strong need to hunt? Well, play is how you help your cat satisfy that need without actually going outside.

Interactive play allows your cat to act out his natural predatory instincts. It's easy and fun to do. Just get one (or two or three or more) of the pole- or wand-style toys that have "prey" (a feather or feathers, thick strips of Mylar, strips of polar fleece, or some other soft item) attached to the end of a string. Then move the prey around so that your cat can hunt it. That means dragging it on the floor, flinging it through the air, dangling it in front of your cat, whatever works to get your cat involved. Your cat will leap after it, chase it, stalk it. The beauty of these interactive toys is that you control where the prey goes, so for your cat it's unpredictable (as prey is in real life). It gives you and your cat quality time together. And it exercises your cat.

The importance of regular, interactive play cannot be overemphasized. You'll see in the chapters of this book that play is suggested as an approach to solving many behavior problems. Regular play can also prevent problems. It doesn't take a lot of time (one or more ten- to fifteen-minute sessions a day) and it really is fun for both of you!

TRAINING

The idea of training a cat somehow seems antithetical to the whole notion of having a cat in your life. Cats have a certain "I don't think so" quality that most cat owners appreciate (or even admire). Yet cats can indeed be trained—as long as positive-reinforcement methods are used. Cats won't put up with the abuse that dogs will. Rather than working to avoid future corrections, cats will just avoid you. That means that traditional correction-based training methods, once so popular in dog training, simply won't work on cats.

You can indeed train your cat if you make it worth his while—that is, you properly motivate your cat to perform the behaviors you seek. Use a clicker (a small plastic box with a flexible piece of metal inside that makes a distinctive *click* when pressed) and you can have a cat who eagerly participates in a training session.

To clicker-train, you pair a click with a food treat. Your cat quickly learns that if he hears the click, a treat is coming. Because a clicker can be so precise, you can clearly mark the behavior you're reinforcing. And your cat will repeat that behavior. That's the building block upon which you end up with a cat who does tricks. Karen Pryor, a pioneer in clicker training, has written a great little book called *Getting Started: Clicker Training for Cats* that spells out the benefits and the how-tos of clicker-training cats.

The beauty of training your cat is not only that you end up with a trained cat, it also opens up a line of communication between the two of you. It provides mental stimulation for your cat—something that many indoor cats are sorely lacking. And it's great for your relationship. In *Getting Started: Clicker Training for Cats*, Pryor writes, "Above all—and this is what makes the method worth trying—clicker transactions can help you and your cat develop a level of communication, understanding and esteem that you may never have imagined possible."

Gentle and Effective Tools to Help With Behavior Problems

FELIWAY®

Since we know that facial pheromones are calming to cats, wouldn't it be nice if we could deposit them wherever and whenever we wanted to calm our feline friends? Well we can, after a fashion. A product called Feliway is a synthetic analog to the feline facial pheromone. Feliway effectively calms cats. It also can help stop spraying, since cats don't spray where they've deposited facial pheromones. It works well to curb scratching, too, since they don't tend to scratch where they have rubbed. Cats also spray and scratch during times of stress, so the calming effects of Feliway are beneficial. The manufacturers of Feliway, which is available through veterinarians and from some pet-supply stores, have backed up their claims through scientific studies.

Throughout this book, you'll see references to Feliway, since it is useful in addressing a variety of behavior problems. It comes in two forms: a spray and a room diffuser. The spray, which is useful for stopping urine marking, is used at least once daily for a month. It can also be sprayed on furniture to help stop inappropriate scratching and in the corners of your cat's carrier, to calm him for travel. The room diffuser is plugged into an outlet, where it diffuses the odorless (to humans) pheromone for a month. If your anxious cat spends much of his time in a single room, this can be very soothing.

TELLINGTON TTOUCH®

Tellington TTouch inventor Linda Tellington-Jones refers to TTouch as "a non-verbal language." The goal of TTouch bodywork is to stimulate the function and vitality of the animal's cells and activate unused neural pathways to the brain. In this way, Tellington TTouch helps change the animal's habitual behavior and emotions.

Circular touches (called TTouches) that are performed on an animal form the centerpiece of the Tellington TTouch system. These touches not only benefit your cat emotionally and behaviorally, they're relaxing for both of you. And they're great for your relationship with your cat. You gain his trust and communicate your love and caring through your touch. With all these advantages, it's worthwhile to make a little effort to learn about TTouch. A new cat-specific book, *TTouch for Your Cat,* is due out in the autumn of 2003. There are also two cat-specific TTouch videos. In addition, you can schedule an appointment with a TTouch practitioner (there are some 250 trained practitioners in the U.S. and Canada, as well as others worldwide). That person will teach you in person how to do TTouch on your cat.

The basic component of the system is the Clouded Leopard circular touch. The other circular touches are variations on the Clouded Leopard. With this touch, you make light circles with your finger pads on the cat's body. Moving just the skin, you start at six o'clock, go all the way around, and end at eight o'clock or nine o'clock. You then move to another spot and do another circle and a quarter. You can keep going until you or your cat is tired of it. (Never force TTouch on your cat—you can encourage him to stay close by extending the arm you're not using for TTouch in a half circle around your cat, but not holding him. If he walks away, let him. But be prepared for him to come back for more.)

The other important TTouch doesn't include a circular motion. The Ear TTouch calms and soothes frightened or stressed cats. It also stimulates acupuncture points that benefit the entire body. With the Ear TTouch, you stroke the cat's ear from base to the tip, using a gentle, upward motion. Put the ear between your thumb and forefinger (with the thumb on top of the ear) and gently stroke. Lift your hand off the ear before starting another stroke and cover every inch of the cat's ear. The Ear TTouch also helps cats who have suffered trauma or who are going into shock. In those cases, perform the Ear TTouch—with a firm touch and quick stroke—on the way to the vet's office.

FLOWER REMEDIES

Throughout the book, flower remedies are suggested to help address the emotions of cats (and owners) in various situations. Developed seventy years ago by Edward Bach, a homeopath and physician, flower remedies, also known as flower essences, use tiny amounts of plant material from specific flowers soaked in water (the flowers are then discarded) and preserved, usually in brandy. The remedies are used to heal on an emotional-spiritual level. Specific flower remedies are used to treat specific emotional issues (like jealousy or anxiety), while various combination products, like the popular "Rescue Remedy"—a combination of five flower essences—tend to have a more general use. Several companies make flower essences, including Bach, Anaflora, Green Hope Farm, and Flower Essence Services. Anaflora and Green Hope Farm make essences specifically for animals, though those developed for humans can be used on your cat. They're safe and can be quite effective.

Typically, the easiest way to administer flower essences to your cat is by putting three or four drops of it in his drinking water. Other methods include rubbing a couple of drops on his ears, putting a few drops into a mister full of water and misting it around the cat, and putting some on his food or a treat. Often it is helpful to take the same essence as your cat, particularly if the emotional issue involves both of you.

MANAGEMENT

Since cats don't respond well to punishment and pretty much do as they please, how do we get them to do what we want? The key is making what we want them to do something they want to do. We can do that through training and rewards. But we also have another potent tool at our disposal: management. In this context, management refers to manipulating the situation so that our cats can't do what we don't want. For example:

- *You don't want your cat licking the butter on the dining-room table?* Use a covered butter dish.

- *Your cat rummages through the trash?* Put the trash in a closet or use bungee cords to keep the lid on the can.

- *You don't want your cat sleeping on the guest bed?* Keep the door to the guest room closed.

Sometimes it takes a little more effort to manage a situation than it might to just yell at your cat every time he does something you don't like. But that yelling is stressful for both of you. It's frustrating when your cat doesn't "obey" you, but if you adjust your expectations that he should, and help him stay out of trouble through management, life with your cat becomes more pleasant.

Throughout this book you'll find tips on general care and problem solving based on communication, management, respect, and love. You don't need to have an adversarial relationship with your cat in order to live together comfortably. If you respect your cat for who he is, and treat him accordingly, you can live together in peace and harmony.

General Care of Your Cat

Caring for your cat requires more than providing food and a litter box. As aloof as they might seem at times, cats require your companionship and attention. And they need a clean litter box, good food, exercise, and veterinary care, at the very minimum. If you want to maximize your enjoyment of your cat, you'll develop a true relationship with her. To do that, you need to spend time with her, focus on her needs, listen to what she is telling you, and learn to understand her. You should appreciate your cat for being the unique thinking, feeling feline that she is.

Make your cat a full-fledged member of the family: be patient with her and give her the benefit of the doubt, like you would any other family member. Focus on the positive and try to just ignore the negative. Don't expect her to do things that are completely against her nature (like using a dirty litter box). You'll reap huge benefits from getting to know your cat as an individual and letting her become a big part of your life.

chapter one

Allergies to Cats

Monica lives with four cats, despite having been diagnosed with allergies to cat dander. Yet she's not walking around sniffling and sneezing all the time and she gives her cats full run of the house. How does she do it? Through a combination of regular grooming, housecleaning, air filtration, and common sense. Even though she still does sneeze occasionally, her love for her cats outweighs the mild discomfort.

Many cats are given up because a family member is allergic to them. In a survey conducted under the auspices of the National Council on Pet Population Study and Policy, "allergies" was cited as the second-most-prevalent reason for relinquishing a cat to a shelter in the United States (after "too many in the house"). But allergies shouldn't mean that a cat has to be given up. Before even considering giving up a cat, an allergic person should first try some methods that might keep the allergies at bay.

WHAT YOUR CAT IS TRYING TO TELL YOU

- *"I'm not trying to make you sick."* Obviously, it's not your cat's fault if you're allergic to him.

- *"Don't give me up."* If you or a family member becomes allergic to your cat, there are many steps you can take before you should consider giving her up.

HOW TO SAY IT

- *Try to keep your cats out of the bedroom.* Reduce the stress on your body by giving yourself an allergen-free night's rest every night. Put your cats in their own, comfortable room, perhaps one with a human bed in it. If you simply can't exile your cats, try putting a heating pad or pads at the foot of the bed to attract your cats away from your pillow.

- *Use an air filter.* A high-grade filter, like a HEPA filter, can help clean the air of the allergens. Get one for your bedroom and for other rooms where you spend time with your cat. Another air purifier that some people with allergies have found effective is the air ionizer, which doesn't use a filter but rather uses electrostatic precipitation to purify the air.

- *Brush your cat regularly.* Getting the hair off the cats and into the brush so that it can't float around in the air can help. If possible, delegate the task to a nonallergic family member. If not, wear a mask while you're doing it.

- *Wipe down your cat.* Premoistened cloths like Pal's Quick Cleansing Wipes can be effective in removing saliva and dander from your cat's hair. Rub your cat with the cloth after combing her. Rub in both directions so that the skin is dampened. These cloths contain natural, food-grade ingredients that shouldn't harm your cat when licked off. Wiping the cat is a lot less stressful (for both of you) than bathing her.

- *Get some help for yourself.* An allergist can probably provide allergy medications that will help you. An alternative practitioner can help you with acupuncture, Chinese herbs, or NAET (Nambrudipad's Allergy Elimination Techniques), a Chinese-medicine-based treatment for treating allergies in both humans and animals.

- *Vacuum frequently.* Use a vacuum cleaner with an air filter on it—and use double or microfilter vacuum bags so that the allergens aren't blown right back out into the room. Vacuum, rather than sweep, bare floors. If the situation is dire, rip up the carpet and have bare floors instead. Carpeting allows dander to accumulate much more than do bare floors.

- *Declutter your house.* The more items in your house to collect dust and dander, the harder it will be for your allergies.

- *Wash your hands after you handle your cat.* This way you can prevent yourself from spreading the dander.

- *Clean the litter box frequently—but get someone else to do it.* Cat urine contains allergens, so you don't want it to languish in the litter box. But you also don't want to handle it, so delegate litter-box duty to nonallergic family members. If that's not possible, consider getting a self-scooping litter box, like the Littermaid, to minimize your exposure to used litter. Wear a mask whenever you handle the litter.

- *Spray your house.* Antiallergen sprays like Allersearch ADS sprayed on furniture and carpet can deactivate the allergens in your home. Allersearch ADS is derived from tannic acid and is considered non-toxic.

- *Improve your cat's diet.* If your cat's coat is in better shape, she'll produce less dander and cause fewer problems for people with allergies. Consider switching to a home-prepared diet, or to a higher-quality commercial food. Some cat owners who feed their cats a raw diet have reported that allergic people tend to have a milder reaction to them. (See the chapter "Diet: What to Feed" for more information.)

HOW NOT TO SAY IT

- *Don't sleep with your cat.* This might be the most important step you take in reducing your allergic reaction. Give your body a rest from the allergens by having her sleep outside your bedroom.

- *Don't hurry to give up your cat.* Try some of the previous suggestions before making the painful decision to find your cat a new home. Your allergy problem may not be as unsolvable as you think.

- *Don't get rid of your cat out of concern for your baby's health if you become pregnant.* Research has shown that children who live with two or more dogs or cats as infants are less likely to develop any type of common allergies, as compared to children raised without pets.

chapter two

Babies and Children

When Lillian and Marcus found out they were expecting a baby, they were overjoyed. For five years, their "baby" had been their cat, Foster, and now they were expanding their family further. Being devoted cat owners, the couple wanted to keep Foster, of course, but they were worried: they'd been warned by several people that it's not safe to keep a cat around a baby.

Cats get a bad rap when it comes to babies. The myth of cats sucking the breath out of babies is unfounded. You can certainly keep your cat when a baby joins your family. But you can make the whole process easier for your cat by preparing him for the impending arrival. It's also imperative that you teach your kids how to behave around cats.

WHAT YOUR CAT IS TRYING TO TELL YOU

- *"What about me?"* For a cat who is used to having his humans' undivided attention, the addition of a baby (or even a visit from a child) can be difficult.

- *"I still have the same needs."* Even if you're busy with a new baby, your cat needs your care and attention. Try to work out a schedule so your cat isn't neglected.

- *"Everything's changing so fast."* Use the months you have to prepare for a baby to help your cat get ready, too. If you're going to be changing the rules, start early so that your cat is accustomed to them by the time the baby arrives.

HOW TO SAY IT

- *Prepare your cat for the changes.* Get him used to the smell of a baby by wearing baby powder yourself. Get him used to the sound of a baby by recording a baby's cry and playing the recording, at low volume—gradually increasing it to full baby wail—while you're pregnant. (You can buy a CD of baby cries for this purpose. See the appendix for ordering information.) If you have any friends with infants, ask them to bring the baby over so that your cat can be around one.

- *Decide what any new rules need to be.* A new baby may mean you need to change the rules for your cat. For example, if your cat is allowed to jump on your lap at any time, you probably won't want her to do that when you have a baby in your lap. So you'll need to teach your cat now that she must sit next to you. Remember, you're changing your cat's life, so try to stay patient. When your cat jumps on your lap, say "Oops!" and put her where you want her, then reward her. You're changing the rules on her, so be gentle and patient.

- *Bring home a baby blanket or cap before you bring home the baby.* Let your cat smell the blanket, to make the arrival of the baby more familiar.

- *Try some Feliway.* This simulated facial pheromone can be calming for your cat. If your cat is stressed by the preparations for the baby, or by the baby's arrival, spraying Feliway, or using it in a diffuser, can be helpful.

- *Set up a safe zone for your cat.* If you don't have one already, set up a room where your cat's bed, litter box, and food dishes are (with the litter box at the opposite side of the room). That can be your cat's safe room, where he can go to get away from the baby (and the child, as time goes by). If you have a toddler, put up a baby gate so that he can't violate your cat's safe zone.

- *Tell your cat about the new baby.* Let her in on the big secret (by talking out loud to her about it) and she may be less surprised by the arrival of the new bundle.

- *Keep to your routines.* Feed your cat on schedule, even when your own schedule seems to have been turned upside down by the baby. Play with your cat as usual, groom him, and try to keep his life as normal as possible.

- *Introduce the baby and the kitty after both have eaten.* They'll both be more placid and content then.

- *Be calm during introductions.* When your cat meets a new baby for the first time (or a child, for that matter), stay relaxed. Your cat takes her cue from you, so if you act tense about that first meeting (and subsequent interactions), she may view the baby with some wariness. Be upbeat and praise your cat for her pleasant attention to the baby. If she ignores the little bundle, that's okay, too.

- *Visualize a good relationship between your cat and the baby.* Send mental pictures to your cat of the two of them peacefully enjoying each other's company.

- *Buy some safety gear.* Block your cat from jumping into the crib by covering it with a safety net (see the appendix for sources) or installing a screen door at the door of the nursery. Or simply close the nursery door when you're not in the baby's room (and use a baby monitor).

- *If you're concerned about your cat trying to snuggle with your baby while you sleep, attach a collar with a bell to your cat.* That way, if he jumps into the baby's crib, you'll hear it.

- *Train the kids.* Teach your kids how to behave around cats. They should learn to recognize when a cat has had enough attention, and they should know not to hold a cat against her will, not to corner a cat, and not to bother a cat when she's eating, sleeping, or using the litter box. They need to be taught how to pick up a cat properly (don't let the poor cat dangle as the child holds her under the arms). They need to respect the cat's eating and litter box as her personal space, where she should never be bothered. Teach them to always treat cats with gentle kindness.

■ *Listen to your cat when he's interacting with small children.* If your cat tells you—by swishing his tail, hissing, growling, or putting his ears back—that he's not comfortable with the child's attention, then tell your child to stop what she's doing immediately. Teach your child these signs and caution her to heed them.

■ *Keep your cat's nails trimmed if you are concerned about the cat scratching the baby or children.* See the chapter on nail trimming for information on the procedure.

HOW NOT TO SAY IT

■ *Don't get rid of your cat because you're going to have a baby.* Unfortunately, the myth lives on that cats will harm babies and that pregnant women can't be around cats. It's true that pregnant women shouldn't handle cat feces, because of the risk of toxoplasmosis, but other family members can help with litter-box duties. Cats don't suck the breath out of babies. Babies (and small children) can live together safely and peacefully.

■ *Don't worry about the effects of cats on your child's allergies.* Recent studies have shown that living with more than one cat or dog as a baby actually decreases the chances that a child will develop any type of common allergies later in life.

■ *Don't allow your cat to be alone with babies and small kids.* Supervision is essential; one mistake on the part of a child—if he corners the cat or tries to hold her against her will—and the cat could bite or scratch the child. Even declawed cats can cause injury with their hind feet or their teeth. Teach your children how to behave around cats, but don't trust them to behave 100 percent of the time. Supervise them.

- *Don't blame the cat.* If your cat reacts to the changes in the house by misbehaving, recognize it for the reaction that is it, and do your best to calm your cat.

- *Don't banish your cat to the garage, laundry room, or basement.* Remember, he didn't choose for you to have kids. With proper training and supervision, your cat and your kids can learn to get along.

- *Don't let your cat lick the baby.* Your cat may want to lavish attention on the baby, but her sandpaper tongue could actually hurt tender baby skin. If she starts trying to groom the baby, distract her with a toy or a treat. Similarly, you don't want her kneading the baby, since she could accidentally scratch him.

- *Don't declaw your cat for fear he'll hurt the baby.* Declawing, which is really amputation, is not necessary or kind. (See the chapter on declawing.) Instead, carefully supervise your cat's interaction with your child and keep your cat's nails trimmed in case he tries to use them.

chapter three

Basic Equipment for Your Cat

Cats are relatively low-maintenance pets, but if you and your cat are going to be happy together, you have to supply some basic amenities to keep him comfortable. Your cat's needs go beyond food, water, and shelter. A happy cat needs to play, to scratch, and to eliminate comfortably. It's easy to provide for those basic needs.

WHAT YOUR CAT IS TRYING TO TELL YOU

- *"Help me be a great companion."* If you want your cat to be a happy, anxiety-free pet, you'll need to spend time with her. Interactive play sessions with toys on strings, kitty "fishing poles," and so forth are extremely important.

- *"I need a clean litter box."* Your cat needs a clean, fresh-smelling place to eliminate. Make sure your litter box is in a location your cat likes, that he approves of the litter you're using, and, most of all, that you scoop and clean the litter box regularly—at least daily. Also be sure that your litter box is large enough and that there are enough of them in your house

- *"A cat's gotta scratch."* If you don't provide your cat with an appropriate place to scratch, she'll find her own—and you might not like what she chooses.

- *"Keep me safe."* Be sure to minimize the hazards inside the house and keep your cat safe when you're outdoors together.

HOW TO SAY IT

Before you bring your new cat home, stock up on the basics:

- *An appropriate litter box (see the chapter on not using the litter box).* Some cats prefer a covered litter box, but many do not. Start out with an uncovered one and see how your cat does. You might want to get a mat to put beneath the litter box, in case your cat kicks litter out of the box. And of course you'll need litter and a scoop.

- *Scratching post.* A cat needs to scratch in order to help maintain his claws and also to stretch his back muscles. Some cats prefer to scratch on vertical posts, while others prefer horizontal. Try both and see which your cat prefers. Sisal is a good covering for the scratching post. The scratching post should have a heavy base so that your cat won't tip it over. Be sure to place it where your cat will use it—many cats like to scratch right after they eat, so placing the post near the food bowl might be wise.

- *Food and water bowls.* Avoid plastic bowls, which are porous and harder to clean completely. Make sure the water bowl is bottom heavy and not easily tipped over. Think about where you want your cat to eat. Be sure it's in a place where your cat will feel safe. Make sure each cat has her own food bowl.

- *High-quality food.* See the chapter "Diet: What to Feed" for a discussion of what makes a food high quality.

- *Interactive toys.* Daily play sessions with your cat are essential, and they're fun, too! Get at least one toy on a string so that you can help your cat act like a predator and make the "prey" move. Be sure to put away the interactive toys when you're not playing with them, since string can be dangerous if your cat swallows it.

- *Toys for the cat to play with by herself.* Give your cat easy access to safe cat toys—Ping-Pong balls, furry mice, and the like—so she can play by herself when the mood strikes her. Cats have preferences about what they think is fun to play with. But don't let your cat get into a rut—try introducing new types of toys every now and then. Most cats love catnip toys, but the allure can wear off. Use catnip toys as a special treat; bring them out only once or twice a week to keep the power of the catnip alive.

- *A brush and comb.* Grooming your cat regularly will help eliminate shed fur in the house. And it will reduce the number of hairballs your cat will hack up. Especially if your cat has medium or long hair, combing or brushing is essential. See the chapter on brushing and combing.

- *A bed.* Your cat should have a comfy place to call his own. Buy him a snuggly cat bed. He may not use it—cats are good at making their own beds. But it's nice to have it available to him. He's more likely to use it if you put it on top of something rather than on the floor.

- *Treats.* Reward your cat's desirable behavior with a tasty morsel. If you decide you'd like to train your cat, treats will be indispensable. See the chapter on healthy treats for some ideas.

- *A carrier for safe travel.* You may not plan to take trips with your cat, but you will have to take her in the car sometimes, even if it's just for short trips to the vet. She shouldn't be loose in the car—that can be dangerous for both of you. Get her a safe carrier—either a hard-sided crate or a soft-sided case (like the Sherpa Bag or the SturdiBag)—for trips. You'll need a carrier for each cat so that you have a safe way to move the cats in case of an emergency. (See the chapter on carriers.)

- *A collar and identification tag.* When your cat is outside the house, he should be wearing an ID tag. If your cat goes outside unsupervised, be sure to use a breakaway collar so that the collar can't get hung on something and choke him. If you're just taking your cat to the vet, a regular collar will work. Add a leash to keep him even safer.

■ *A baby gate if you're going to be introducing the cat into a household with dogs.* If you have an inquisitive dog, a baby gate across the door of the room where your cat's food and litter box are will allow your cat to keep a distance and approach the dog at her own pace. The gate will allow your dog to see the cat, without being right in the cat's face. See the chapter on dogs and cats.

■ *Nail clippers.* It's important to clip your cat's nails to keep them from growing so long that they cut into his pads. Trimming his nails also helps minimize any damage from scratching. Get clippers that are designed for use with cats, or use human nail clippers if that works more easily for you. See the chapter on nail trimming.

HOW NOT TO SAY IT

■ *Don't wing it.* Take a shopping trip before you bring your cat home for the first time. You'll want your cat to know immediately where his litter box is. He'll need fresh water right away. And he might want to retreat straight to his new bed.

■ *Don't skimp on your cat.* She's not "just a cat." Your new feline family member has needs that it's up to you to meet.

chapter four

Bringing Your New Cat Home

Linda was so excited by the prospect of adopting a new cat. But when she brought Eli home from the shelter, she was disappointed because he hid from her for a week. She tried pulling him out from under the bed, but he hissed and struggled. Both of them were unhappy and Linda was afraid Eli would never be the companion she was seeking.

As excited as you might be by the new arrival, slow and easy is the name of the game when it comes to introducing a new cat into the household. Whether or not you have other pets in the family, you'll want to give your new cat some space of his own and let him acclimate himself to his new situation at his own pace.

WHAT YOUR CAT IS TRYING TO TELL YOU

- *"I need to get the lay of the land."* An unfamiliar house can be overwhelming to a cat. Many cats will stake out a small space on their own and huddle there until they're ready to explore.

- *"Who are these strange animals?"* If you have other pets, they might be very frightening to your new cat—even if they haven't actually met.

- *"Where's my stuff?"* Be sure to give your cat easy access to food, water, a litter box, and a place to scratch. It's very important that your cat know where to eliminate.

- *"Give me some space."* Your cat might want some time alone. Or he might want to share time with you in a room, without your hands on him. Take your cues from your cat.

HOW TO SAY IT

- *Create a safe room.* Before your bring your new cat home, set up a room for her that she can call her own at the beginning. It can be a spare bedroom or a bathroom. Put the cat's food and water bowls, her litter box, and something to scratch in the room, as well as a comfy place to sleep and a safe toy or two.

- *Bring your cat right into the safe room.* As soon as you enter the house, hustle him right into the safe room, keeping him in his carrier. Once the door is closed, open the carrier and let him come out of it at his own pace. If he doesn't want to come out at all, that's just fine. He will eventually. If he does come out, pet him and talk to him, depending on his desires. Then leave him to explore on his own.

- *Use Feliway in the safe room.* This simulated facial pheromone will make your cat feel more comfortable. Either use a Feliway room diffuser or spray it at cat-nose height on prominent areas in the room—the places a cat would naturally rub against to deposit facial pheromones. Spray a single squirt in those spots once or twice a day until you notice your cat rubbing on those objects herself.

- *Read to your cat.* If your cat needs his space and hides under the bed or walks away when you try to pet him, just try being with him and talking to him. Try reading aloud to him, just to get him used to the sound of your voice.

- *Do TTouch on all your cats.* Gentle TTouch circles will help build you bond with your new cat. And they will help keep your resident cats less stressed over the new arrival. Eventually, after you've introduced the cats, you can, with the help of an assistant, do TTouches on the cats at the same time, in the same room, to help them feel more comfortable around one another.

■ *Take your cat to the veterinarian before introducing her to other cats in your home.* You want to ensure that the new family member doesn't have any infectious diseases. See the chapter on going to the veterinarian for more information on the actual visit.

■ *Introduce your other pets gradually.* After your new cat is comfortable in his safe room—and this may take a few days—it is time to start introducing the other pets.

Introductions to resident cats:

■ *Cats are very territorial, which is why it is so important to introduce the newcomer gradually.* One way you can do this is to bring a blanket or towel out of the safe room so that your resident cat can smell the scent of the new cat. Do this well before you make any face-to-face introductions. You should also bring into the safe room items that carry your resident cat's scent (bedding, for example). This will help them become accustomed to each other's smell before they actually meet.

■ *Switch rooms.* Bring out the new cat and let the resident cats into the safe room and close the door. Let the new cat explore other areas of the house. By the time they meet face-to-face, they won't be complete strangers.

Introductions to resident dogs:

■ *Put up a baby gate on the door of the safe room.* That way, the dog won't be able to get in but the animals can interact a little. And the cat can always hop over (or under) the gate to meet his new friend. See the chapter on dogs and cats for more information on creating harmony between the two species.

■ *Whether you have dogs, cats, or no other pets at all, gradually make new rooms accessible to your new cat.* If your house's layout allows, open up more rooms to your cat, one at a time. This will keep the stress to a minimum.

■ *Be patient.* If you want to avoid stress-related problems with your new cat (these problems can range from destruction to not using the litter box and even to health problems), your cat should get to know her new house and family at her own pace. It can be difficult when you're eager for your cat to be a full-fledged family member. But a little patience at this juncture can translate into a lifetime of happiness.

■ *Take your clues from your cat.* You may not need to go as slowly as this chapter is suggesting. If your cat is the adventurous sort, give him access to more of the house more quickly, if he seems to be ready for it. Just don't rush him into anything.

HOW NOT TO SAY IT

■ *Don't isolate your new cat.* It's important for your new cat to have time to herself in her safe room, but you need to spend time with her in there as well. Talk to her, and to the extent she'll allow, play with her, stroke her, even brush her.

■ *Don't neglect your resident pets either.* They need your attention now more than ever.

■ *Don't force yourself on your cat.* You should spend time with your new cat, but you don't have to be in his face about it. Some cats will take refuge under the bed and refuse to come out. If your cat is under the bed, get down on the floor, raise the bed skirt, if you have one, and talk to him. See if he wants you to scratch him while he's down there. Respect his comfort zone: if he turns his back on you, get up off the floor and just talk to him from a safe distance. Try reading aloud—it'll get him familiar with your voice and scent. Eventually, he'll come to you.

■ *Don't expect your resident cats to embrace the newcomer (or vice versa).* Cats are very territorial, which is why it is necessary to introduce them gradually.

- *Don't switch food and litter too quickly.* For the sake of your new cat's comfort and stability, leave him on the food he was eating when he came to your house and try to use the same type of kitty litter. He doesn't have to stay on these things for life, but you can decrease stress by keeping these familiar items in his life.

- *Don't punish your new cat for infractions.* It's never a good idea to shout at a cat, or spray him with water, but it's particularly important at this special time for your cat to build positive associations with you. If you see your cat doing something you don't like (for example scratching the furniture), address the problem gently and properly (by supplying a scratching post, in this instance. See the chapter on clawing the furniture for solutions to this particular problem).

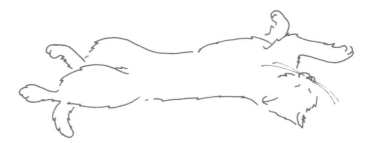

chapter five

Brushing and Combing

The beautiful long hair of Trisha's long-haired cat, Audrey, quickly becomes matted. Unfortunately, Audrey doesn't enjoy being combed (probably because she's matted) and each grooming session with Trisha turns into a battle. Trisha ends up having her cat shaved down periodically to get rid of the mats.

Brushing or combing your cat shouldn't be a chore. It can and should be an enjoyable ritual that both you and your cat look forward to. Taking care of your cat's coat is an important part of being a good cat owner. Not only is it important to your cat's health (it cuts down on hairballs) and comfort (mats hurt!), it can build the bond between the two of you. Plus, it reduces shedding and hairballs. If brushing or combing hasn't become a daily ritual for you and your cat, you can help make the procedure more pleasant with some patience, kindness, and a little food.

WHAT YOUR CAT IS TRYING TO TELL YOU

- *"Ouch!"* If you delay brushing so long that your cat is tangled or matted, brushing can actually hurt. No wonder he doesn't like it.

- *"This is tedious."* If your grooming session goes on too long, your cat can get bored and want to walk away. Keep your sessions short and enjoyable.

- *"What's in it for me?"* Some cats need a little extra motivation to participate in a grooming session. Time to break out the treats.

- *"Ahhhhh."* Brushing should feel good. Properly done, with the right equipment and frequency, your cat will luxuriate in a brushing session.

HOW TO SAY IT

- *Approach the task with a positive attitude.* Your mood sets the tone for the session. So go into it feeling upbeat and confident that both you and your cat will enjoy the brushing. Keep the grooming session positive—even if you're tempted to lose your patience.

- *Groom with your hands first.* Anitra Frazier, a professional cat groomer and author of *The New Natural Cat,* suggests that you start every grooming session by grooming with your hands. Stroke every part of your cat to communicate what it is you're about to do. While you're doing it, think about how pleasant it's going to be for him.

- *Use the right equipment.* There are several types of brushes and combs, each appropriate for certain types of coats. Be sure you choose the right comb and brush for your cat.

- *Do TTouch with the grooming equipment.* Make gentle circles on your cat with the brush or the comb to help alleviate any anxiety or discomfort surrounding the tool. You can also do small TTouches with your fingers around any matted areas to alleviate hypersensitivity to the mats.

- *Groom from head to toe.* Brush in the direction of your short-haired cat's coat. Long-haired cats should be combed.

- *Be patient and gentle.* If your cat doesn't settle down during the grooming session, don't get mad. End the session, then start up again later (but not too much later). Short, easy sessions are the way to go.

- *Start young.* Start grooming your cat as soon as you acquire him. If he's a kitten, all the better, though he's never too old to learn to be groomed. You want to condition him to having his body touched and groomed.

- *Listen to your cat.* If your cat objects to anything, stop. When your cat says the session's over, end it. Even if you haven't finished, don't push her past her limit. Always end the session on a positive note.

- *Brush frequently.* The more often you groom your cat's coat, the easier it will be on the cat. A long-haired cat should be combed daily so that you never encounter mats and so that your cat doesn't ingest so much fur during self-grooming that he throws it up. (Daily brushing can cut down on hairballs in short-haired cats, too.) Take advantage of this quality time together.

- *Start from scratch.* If your cat is very matted, it might be easier for you to have a professional grooming, which might require a shaving. Once she's mat-free, start brushing her regularly so that you never have to shave her again.

- *Reward good behavior.* Be sure to reward your cat for letting you groom him. The brushing itself might be a reward. But if there's hesitation, bring out some treats.

- *Watch your cat's tail.* If it starts to twitch as you're grooming, know that she might be getting annoyed and that the grooming session might have to come to an end. Work quickly and gently to get as much done as you can.

- *If you use a grooming table or stand your cat on the floor to brush, put down a nonstick mat.* That way, your cat won't lose his footing. This should make him feel more comfortable with the grooming.

- *Talk to your cat.* All the while you're brushing and combing, talk to your cat in calm, sweet tones. Tell her what you're doing and why. Use this time to build your connection.

The Right Tool for the Job

Selecting the right brush for your cat's coat is very important. Here's a guide:

Short-haired cats:

- Rubber curry comb or Zoom Groom
- Slicker brush
- Fine-toothed comb
- Flea comb (during flea season, if your cat goes outdoors or lives with dogs who do)

Long-haired cats:

- Wide- and medium-toothed combs (start with the wide)
- Round-tipped mat-splitting scissors (or other mat-breaking device). Be sure to learn to use mat breakers properly and never try to cut a mat out with regular scissors.

Author Anitra Frazier, a professional cat groomer, supplies detailed instructions on grooming your cat in her book *The New Natural Cat.*

- *Put your hands all over his body.* Check your cat regularly for lumps, swelling, wounds, or abrasions. Talk to your vet if you find anything suspicious. If you're checking regularly, you're likely to detect signs of disease very early, which is as important for cats as it is for humans.

- *Try some flower essences.* If your cat is stressed by grooming, or if you anticipate a particularly stressful grooming session, give him some Rescue Remedy to calm him.

- *Learn from an expert.* If you have any questions about the best technique to use to brush your particular type of cat, stop into a grooming shop for advice. Bring a picture of your cat. If you have a pedigreed cat, talk to his breeder about how best to groom him, if possible.

HOW NOT TO SAY IT

- *Don't hurt your cat.* A brush can cause pain, if too much pressure is exerted or if it's not the right brush for the cat's coat. If you pull on a mat with a comb, it can really hurt. Take it slow and easy and be sure that you're using the right equipment. Keep an eye out for any sign of discomfort or pain.

- *Don't turn grooming into a battle.* If your cat won't sit still, end the session and start later. Next time be ready to give a treat for even a hint of tolerance and keep rewarding as long as the session lasts. Try grooming when your cat is pooped out or in a mellow mood.

- *Don't groom anywhere your cat is not allowed.* It saves your back to put your cat on an elevated surface, like the kitchen counter. But if your cat is not allowed to jump on the counter, you're sending a confusing message. A grooming table might be the answer.

chapter six

Care of the Aging Cat

As Dorothy's cat, Herman, started becoming geriatric (he's already fifteen), Dorothy noticed that he was putting on weight. He no longer tore through the house or used his scratching post daily. Dorothy's friend Amy also had an aging cat, Daisy, who is sixteen. In comparing notes, the two discovered that their cats were aging very differently. Daisy lost weight and ate less. She became a little cranky—she was now likely to walk away from the nightly petting routine she once demanded. Herman, on the other hand, became more affectionate with age.

A well-cared-for cat can live a long time. Cats, like people, tend to change with age, and the way they change can vary. Geriatric cats require a little extra TLC and consideration and maybe some extra veterinary care. But as they grow old, each day becomes precious, so the extra effort is well worth it.

WHAT YOUR CAT IS TRYING TO TELL YOU
- *"My senses aren't what they used to be."* In some cats, one or more of their senses decline with age. They may not see, hear, or smell as acutely. Some cats go totally blind or deaf.

- *"I get chilly."* Older cats can have trouble regulating their body temperatures, so they may seek out warm spots in your house.

- *"I can't keep myself as beautiful as I once did."* Older cats frequently have difficulty grooming themselves carefully. They can lose flexibility and have trouble reaching certain areas of their body. Your senior citizen may need a little extra grooming help from you.

- *"I need you."* Your aging cat might need some extra care from you. After a lifetime together, surely he's earned this special attention.

HOW TO SAY IT

- *Keep your aging cat in the house.* Chances are if you have a cat who has lived into her teens, she already spends most, if not all, of her time indoors. But if your cat's senses have started to decline with age, you really should insist she stay inside, because she's at a real disadvantage. She can go outside with you, but you need to be there with her to keep her out of danger.

- *Be sure to take your cat in for regular wellness exams.* Routine blood work can reveal addressable problems before your cat shows symptoms. While this is good practice throughout the life of your cat, it's especially important if he is geriatric.

- *Keep your cat's life on an even keel.* As your cat ages, she's less able to tolerate changes in her routine and she's also more vulnerable to stress. (Stress can be very hard on cats, leading to a depressed immune system and an increased likelihood of illness.) Go out of your way to keep up with your cat's routine. Avoid introducing any major life changes, when possible.

- *Do TTouch ear work on your older cat every day.* Ear work stimulates acupuncture points in the ears that benefit the whole body. It also helps stimulate digestion and is easy for sensitive older cats to accept. The touches should be soft—Linda Tellington-Jones suggests that you "imagine you are stroking rose petals."

- *Keep your eye on your cat's teeth.* Tartar buildup and gum disease can pose a real health risk for your cat. Not only can it make it difficult for your cat to chew, but it can also release bacteria into the bloodstream. If you see signs of problems, like yellow or brown teeth or puffy, inflamed gums, talk with your veterinarian about the advisability of a teeth cleaning. Be sure that diagnostic blood work is done prior to your cat being put under anesthesia to rule out any problems that would make the anesthesia more dangerous.

- *Look into nutritional supplements.* If your cat is arthritic, talk to your veterinarian about nutraceuticals. Glucosomine and chondroitin can help ease the pain and inflammation of arthritis, without side effects. One made for cats is called Cosequin. Other similar supplements include Glycoflex for Cats (made from the green-lipped mussel) and SeaFlex. Nutritional supplements with antioxidants, such as Nu-Cat, might be beneficial for your aging cat as well. See the appendix for sources.

- *Adjust your cat's environment to accommodate his limitations.* If your senior citizen can't jump like he once used to, make sure there are things low to the ground for him to jump onto and off of (a sturdy apple crate with a fleece cover, for example). Or get a multitiered cat tree so that he can make short jumps from one level to another. If he has trouble getting on the couch, bed, or his favorite chair, consider putting ramps or steps in front of them. (See the appendix for sources for pet ramps and steps.)

- *Pay close attention to your cat's litter-box use.* More (or less) frequent urination or going outside the box might be signs of diabetes or kidney or urinary tract problems. You should take your cat to the vet if you see these changes, or if there is any blood in the urine, or straining or pain while using the litter box. If your cat is defecating less often, a vet visit is in order, since she may be constipated—again, something more common in older cats.

- *Make sure your cat is drinking—but take note if he starts drinking a lot.* Free, easy access to water is very important to the aging cat. An automatic fountain, like the Petmate Fresh Flow or the Drinkwell, both available at pet-supply stores or through catalogs, provides circulating, filtered water in a little waterfall. It may motivate your cat to drink more often. If your cat starts drinking a great deal more than usual, however, take her to see the veterinarian. This can be a sign of several illnesses, like kidney disease and diabetes.

- *Get a night-light.* Sometimes fading eyesight can make the dark frightening for older cats—and they let you know it by yowling in the night. Plug a night-light into the room where your cat spends most of his night hours and you might prevent that panic from setting in.

- *Keep your cat cozy warm.* If your elderly cat is spending more time around the heat vents or sleeping in sunny spots, help her stay warm by lining her bed with fleece or even buying a heated pet bed.

- *Play with your cat.* Your older cat may seem inactive, but if you use interactive toys, perhaps you can persuade him to play. Even if he's not leaping in the air after the toy like he once did, the play time provides mental challenges and wonderful bonding time for the two of you.

- *Give her some more litter boxes.* If your house has more than one floor, put a litter box on each floor so your cat doesn't have to go too far to use the box. Her bladder control may not be what it used to be. If your cat is used to eliminating outside, establish a box (or two) for her inside so that she doesn't have to make a trip to eliminate. Make sure that the sides of the litter boxes aren't so high that they're difficult for your cat to get into and out of.

- *Groom your older cat regularly.* He might not be able to groom himself as well as he did when he was younger. You can pick up some of the slack through a daily ritual of gentle brushing and combing.

- *Be prepared to nurse your cat at home.* If your elderly cat becomes ill with something like chronic renal failure, she may require special home care that can extend her life. You might have to give her subcutaneous fluids, for example. This special time together can be a very intimate, memorable period in your lives.

■ *Don't chalk up every problem to "old age" and assume your cat can't be helped.* Changes in coat, energy level, weight, appetite . . . all are signs of diseases of old age that a veterinarian can address. If you notice changes in his health or behavior, consult your veterinarian. There may be medication or other therapies that would make him feel better. See the chapter "Signs of Illness" for more symptoms.

■ *Don't automatically vaccinate your elderly cat.* Talk with your veterinarian about whether your cat needs more vaccinations—she's probably been given enough for a lifetime (see the chapter on vaccinations). If your cat's immune system is not at its peak because of aging, the vaccinations might be very hard on her.

■ *Don't overlook weight loss.* It might be a sign of something that needs to be treated, like hyperthyroidism (an overactive thyroid gland), a condition that is fairly common in older cats. It might be something more serious, like renal failure or cancer. Weigh your cat regularly and write down his weight so that you notice a downward trend or any dramatic (over a half pound) weight loss.

■ *Don't ignore even small things.* Cats have evolved to hide their weaknesses. They don't readily let you know when they're ill or in pain. So it's up to you to uncover the little lumps and bumps, the appetite and behavior changes that may be the sign of a health problem. Become good friends with your veterinarian so that you can pick up the phone when you're concerned.

■ *Don't let your cat go without eating.* If your cat's sense of smell isn't good, his appetite may flag. But your cat needs to eat, each and every day. Going without food for even two days can cause fatty liver disease. If your cat's appetite is waning, talk to your veterinarian—you need to find out the cause. If it's a simple case of your cat not smelling the food, you can make your cat's food more enticing. See the chapter on finicky eating for information on food enhancers. Just make sure your cat eats something.

- *Don't let your cat get obese.* If your cat's energy levels decline with age, she'll be burning fewer calories. If she is eating the same amount, she'll get fat (unless her metabolism changes). Obesity can lead to diabetes and a variety of other diseases. It can make arthritis more painful. Don't let that happen. See the chapter on obesity for information on safely reducing your cat's weight. Better yet, keep her active so that it doesn't become a problem.

- *Don't give your cat pain relievers without talking with your veterinarian.* Many pain relievers sold for humans, like acetaminophen (Tylenol) and aspirin, are dangerous to cats. If your cat is in pain from arthritis, talk to your vet about what you can safely give him.

- *Don't mock your cat's limitations.* Just as you would never laugh at an elderly person for stumbling, don't even think of chuckling at your cat if she falls trying to jump from one chair to another, or displays other signs of infirmity. It's disrespectful and disloyal.

- *Don't expect your cat to behave as he did in the prime of life.* When your cat becomes geriatric, you may need to adjust your expectations of him. He might not smell as good. He may not always make it to the litter box. His declining agility might mean he knocks objects off tables. He might get a little cranky sometimes. But he's still your cat, your stalwart companion, who has stuck with you through thick and thin. Be patient with him; cut him a great deal of slack and enjoy every moment you get to share with him.

- *Don't get your elderly cat a kitten to try to keep him young.* This is a decision not to be taken lightly. A new kitten might stress your cat in a way that would be detrimental to his health. Instead, do your part to keep him young by playing with him.

- *Don't hang on too long.* It can be very difficult to say good-bye to a beloved cat, particularly one who has been in your life for a very long time. But if your cat's quality of life is declining precipitously, do some soul-searching about whether he's ready for you to release him. See the chapter on euthanasia for more information.

chapter seven

Carriers

Sparky hated car rides—the only time he was put in the car was to go to the veterinarian. His owner, Ray, kept a flimsy cardboard carrier for Sparky, but the cat yowled inside and bit at the carrier to the point where he could stick his head out. Ray worried that Sparky would escape from the carrier and start racing all over the car, but he never seemed to be able to come up with a better solution for transporting him.

Even if your cat rarely goes anywhere, it's essential that he have a carrier. A carrier is a prerequisite for trips to the veterinarian, any kind of long-distance trip, and for emergency preparedness. It's a safe place to put your cat if the door of your house needs to be propped open, and it's a safe haven he can seek out. Selecting the right carrier is important, as is familiarizing your cat to his carrier so that he's comfortable going into it.

WHAT YOUR CAT IS TRYING TO TELL YOU

- *"This place means trouble."* Many cats never see the inside of the carrier unless something unpleasant, like going to see the veterinarian, is about to happen.

- *"Get me out of here!"* If you don't work to create pleasant associations with the carrier, your cat will continue to view it as a torture chamber.

- *"It's my safe place."* A cat who has become accustomed to his carrier and who is given free access to it can use it as a safe retreat when life gets too hectic.

- *"Let's see if I can get out of this one."* It's important that your carrier be sturdy enough to keep your cat from escaping—as well as strong enough to protect him in case the carrier is dropped or thrown from the car.

HOW TO SAY IT

- *Invest in a strong carrier.* You can buy the plastic kennel-type carrier, like the kind people use with dogs on airplanes. Or you can try one of the lighter nylon carriers, like the Sherpa Bag or SturdiBag. Whichever type you select, make sure it will contain your cat when you travel. The cardboard carriers are useful in a pinch, but probably won't outlive your cat—nor will they keep your cat particularly safe in the event of an accident.

- *Think about how you'll be using the carrier.* If you plan to travel a great deal with your cat, buy a carrier that is lightweight but safe. Both the Sherpa Bag and the SturdiBag can be carried over your shoulder, making them convenient for travel. Make sure whichever carrier you buy will fit under the airline seat in front of you, just in case you need to take your cat with you on a plane.

- *Buckle the carrier in.* If you plan to do a lot of car travel with your cat, buy the type of carrier that you can fasten in with your seat belt. (This is a feature of both the SturdiBag and the Sherpa Bag.) Strapping the carrier in provides an extra measure of safety for car travel.

- *Acclimate your cat to the carrier.* Before you have to use it, put the crate out for your cat to sniff and occasionally toss treats inside. Ideally your cat will wander in and find a tasty surprise. This will do wonders for his associations with the carrier. If your cat is not inclined to go anywhere near the carrier, put some treats near it, then put some more closer to the carrier. Eventually you'll be able to put the treats in the carrier and your cat will go in. Keep it casual. When you see him go in it for the second time, close the door for a few seconds, then let him out and gradually increase the amount of time you ask him to stay in the carrier, rewarding him every step of the way.

- *Use a clicker.* If you clicker-train your cat (see the chapter on clicker training), you can use the clicker to train your cat to go in—and even stay in—her crate. It's a fun and useful application of a fun training method.

- *Try some Feliway.* If your cat isn't entirely comfortable in the carrier, but you need to take him somewhere, try spraying some Feliway in each of the interior four corners of the carrier ten to twenty minutes before you need to travel. This synthetic facial pheromone will make the carrier smell familiar and will have a calming effect.

HOW NOT TO SAY IT

- *Don't force your cat into the crate.* If you can help it, try not to stuff your cat into his crate when you need to go somewhere. Cats are expert at extending their legs and making it very difficult for you to get them inside. It's better if you create positive associations with the carrier so that you can just toss a treat inside to get your cat to go in.

- *Don't reward bad behavior in the carrier.* If your cat starts loudly yowling in her carrier (and you don't enjoy the yowling), don't coo soothing words of sympathy to her. Rather, stay silent during the yowling and wait for a moment of silence. Then praise your cat or give her a treat (if you can do so without opening the crate and tempting her to escape).

- *Don't buy a carrier that is too small.* Your cat should be able to stand up and turn around inside his carrier. Cats can make themselves incredibly small, particularly when they're scared, but if you want your cat to be able to travel comfortably in his carrier, it needs to be large enough for him to stretch out sufficiently. If the carrier is extra large, you can put a small travel litter box in it for long car trips.

- *Don't use the carrier exclusively for vet visits.* Every now and then, take your cat for a short ride in the car to nowhere so she won't assume the worst every time she's put in the carrier.

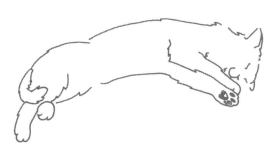

chapter eight

Catnip

Anna's cat, Lionel, is a catnip junkie. Whenever she brings out any of the dried herb, he's all over her. If she sprinkles it on his scratching post, he lolls about in ecstasy, rubbing his body on it as much as he can. The herb truly seems to intoxicate him for ten to fifteen minutes.

What is it about catnip? It's the nepetalactone, the active ingredient in the plant, that cats go ape over. The majority of adult cats react to it. They can easily seem intoxicated just by being around it. Cat owners are lucky to have this enticing substance at their disposal. As long as you don't dilute its power by overusing it, catnip can help you solve your behavior problems by attracting your cat to desirable things and places (like scratching posts).

WHAT YOUR CAT IS TRYING TO TELL YOU

- *"Bring it on!"* If your cat is one who enjoys the catnip, you'll want to ration it out so that he doesn't tire of it.

- *"I'm in heaven."* Catnip seems to put cats into ecstasy.

- *"It tastes good, too."* Many cats enjoy eating catnip—fresh or dried. Catnip-flavored treats are popular as well.

- *"What's the big deal?"* Some cats simply aren't turned on by catnip, so don't even try to force it on them.

HOW TO SAY IT

- *Use catnip to your advantage.* Spice up your cat's life with catnip by sprinkling it in places you want your cat to enjoy, like his scratching post, his cat tree, and his bed. Many cat products now come with a supply of dried catnip to entice the cat to use the product.

- *Try growing your own.* You can plant catnip seeds and grow your own houseplant so that you can give your cat the treat of fresh catnip. (You can also harvest the leaves and dry them.) Be careful to keep the plant completely out of your cat's reach (in a closed room, for instance) or your cat will surely defoliate it.

- *Keep it sealed up.* To keep your cat from raiding the catnip supply, keep dried catnip in a sealed glass container. This will also keep the catnip potent.

- *Refresh her toys with catnip.* If your cat has lost interest in a particular toy, try sprinkling some dried catnip or dip it in a jar of catnip. Do this with plain toys, rather than buying catnip-filled toys, and you won't have to worry about your cat becoming sick of catnip because her catnip-filled toys are always available.

- *Look for a supplier of good catnip.* Since your cat might ingest the catnip, try to find a source of organically grown catnip, to minimize the pesticides he takes in.

- *Try some catnip treats.* There are at least two brands of catnip-flavored treats available, Kookamunga and Cosmic.

■ *Don't overdo the catnip.* Like any item that is available in abundance, catnip will become less attractive if it's always around. Put away all catnip toys and loose catnip. Bring out the catnip no more than every week or so to keep it from losing its potent effect.

■ *Don't bother giving catnip to young cats.* Kittens under the age of about three to six months don't usually respond to it—in fact, they avoid it.

■ *Don't worry about catnip.* As intoxicating as it is, there's no evidence that it's addictive or harmful in any way. So let your cat indulge periodically.

■ *Don't think there's something wrong with your cat if she doesn't like catnip.* Not all cats react to it. If your cat doesn't give a fig about it, there's nothing wrong with her. Up to a third of adult cats don't react to the herb.

chapter nine

Clicker Training Your Cat

Amanda loves to amaze her friends by showing how her tuxedo cat, Dylan, will come when called, sit when asked, give a high five, and even jump through a hoop. Everyone thinks that Dylan is an absolute genius and that Amanda should become a showbiz animal trainer. What Amanda doesn't tell her friends is that training a cat to do tricks is easy—and fun. All it takes is the right equipment, the right motivation for the cat, and a little bit of timing and patience.

Cats are so brilliant that they've convinced humans that they can't be trained. While there aren't that many things most people need their cats to do for them (unlike most dogs, who seem to be asked for a laundry list of behaviors), that doesn't mean we can't train them for fun. Your cat might well enjoy learning to do tricks or even useful tasks, like coming when called or going to his place in the kitchen instead of getting underfoot at mealtime.

The beautiful thing about training your cat is that it helps your relationship. You spend quality time with your cat, your cat gets mental stimulation (which is so important!), and you both have fun. So get out your treats and a clicker and give it a try!

WHAT YOUR CAT IS TRYING TO TELL YOU

■ *"I can be trained—on my terms."* By training your cat with a clicker, you allow him to think he's controlling the game, since his actions determine when you click and give him a treat.

■ *"Let's spend some time together!"* Short training sessions allow you to share some quality time on a daily basis.

■ *"This is fun!"* Teaching your cat to do tricks is fun for both of you. He gets treats, you get to have a cat who does tricks. It's a win-win proposition.

■ *"I'm more than just a pretty face."* Cats are smart. Training allows them to exercise their brains.

■ *"Keep me occupied and maybe I'll stay out of trouble."* If you spend time training your cat, she'll expend both mental and physical energy. Then when she's left to her own devices, perhaps she'll sleep rather than get into mischief.

HOW TO SAY IT

■ *Use a clicker.* A clicker is a small plastic box with a piece of metal in it. When you press the piece of metal, it makes a clicking sound. Couple that click with a food reward and you have a powerful training tool. Cats don't respond well to punishment, which is why traditional dog-training methods (which call for "collar corrections" using choke chains) seem inconceivable for cats. But positive training methods, especially clicker training, work very well for cats. One of the pioneers in developing clicker training for dogs, Karen Pryor, also encourages its use for cats. Her book, *Getting Started: Clicker Training for Cats,* is an easy-to-read and easy-to-follow primer for clicker training your cat. The method is fun and positive and it works!

■ *Teach your cat to target a pencil.* Pryor recommends the first thing you teach your cat with a clicker is to touch a pencil, chopstick, or other similar object with her nose. Hold out the pencil. Your cat will naturally touch her nose to it. As she does that, click on the clicker. Then give her a treat. Move the pencil and do it again. Before long, your cat will move a step or two to touch the pencil. Click and treat each time she touches it. Now you're on your way. You can use the target pencil to lead your cat from one place to another (perhaps through a hoop). Voilà, a cat who follows your lead.

- *Be careful about the first "trick" that you teach.* Clicker-trained animals tend to default to the first behavior they were taught with the clicker. When you bring out the clicker and treats for a training session, they'll start offering behaviors, starting with the first one they've learned. So if that first trick is sitting, for example, it's not much of a springboard for further tricks. Targeting is a very useful trick that makes a great default behavior that you control.

- *Keep your sessions short.* No need to sour your training sessions by making them long and boring. Short sessions—just a minute or two, even—are fun and easy to accomplish several times a day.

- *Use your head (and a clicker) to help solve behavior problems.* Is your cat doing something that you wish he'd stop? Think of something he could do instead, something that's incompatible with the undesirable behavior, and clicker-train him to do that. *Getting Started: Clicker Training for Cats* offers step-by-step instructions for using a clicker to solve several common behavior problems.

- *Teach your cat to come when called.* While cats are famous for not responding when you call, if you use a clicker and treats, you can have a cat who hurries to you on cue. One of the keys to success is to reward your cat each and every time he comes when you call. Start by calling his name. When he's coming reliably, add the word *come* afterward. Then you'll have a strong cue that specifically means "come to me right now and you will get a treat." Remember, never call your cat to come and fail to reward. And never, ever call your cat and get cross with him because he didn't come fast enough. Just give him extra tasty treats for coming quickly.

- *Make your treats delicious.* Your cat might work for mere pieces of kibble. But if she doesn't, up the ante by giving her little bits of tuna, salmon, cheese, or other tasty tidbits. The operative word is *little*. Cats' mouths are very small, so the tiniest treat makes a good reward. You don't want to fill your cat up on treats or make her fat. Try to keep the treats as healthy as possible. See the chapter on healthy treats for ideas.

- *Keep it fun.* Teach your cat to do fun things that will amuse and challenge both of you. Some ideas include:

  - Sit on cue
  - Spin
  - High five or wave
  - Jump through a hoop
  - Jump from one piece of furniture to another

- *Use your imagination.* Think of hands-off ways you can get your cat to perform the desired behaviors. Targeting is a great start (she can follow the pencil to spin, for example: click after the spin is accomplished and work on it until she spins without following the target). Capturing is another method: keep a clicker handy and click and treat when your cat does something especially cute, like showing you her belly. Do it often enough and she'll start offering the behavior for a click.

- *Have a plan.* Set some training goals so you don't get stuck in a rut.

- *Do some reading.* Read Karen Pryor's book and join the great Cat-Clicker e-mail list on the Internet, run by clicker trainer Wendy Jeffries (see the appendix for subscription information). Both will provide invaluable assistance and also spark ideas for things you can train your cat to do.

HOW NOT TO SAY IT

- *Don't lose your patience.* You're doing this for the fun of it. Don't turn it into a speed challenge. Do brief sessions daily (or more than once a day) and keep them lighthearted and fun. If your cat doesn't seem to be catching on to something you want him to do, get creative and think about new ways to teach the behavior. Turn it into a fun challenge.

- *Don't rush to add a cue.* Once you've taught your cat a trick—and she's done it enough times in a row that you're confident that she'll perform it again—then it's time to add the cue. If the trick is targeting, for example, say "Touch" (or whatever word you choose) just before the cat touches the pencil—but only after so many repetitions that you know she will do it. That's a surefire way for your cat to associate the cue with the behavior—and is much easier (for both cats and dogs) than the traditional dog-training method of saying a word your pet doesn't understand, then making her do it.

- *Don't physically place your cat where you want him.* Pushing him into a "down," for example, does not promote cooperation. Instead, lure him into a down or capture the behavior with a click and treat when he lies down on his own.

- *Don't reprimand your cat.* Training a cat is all about having fun. If you're expecting your cat to do one thing and she does another, don't yell at her. Instead, ignore the undesired behavior and wait until you get the behavior you want. Then click and treat. Train your cat by rewarding her for doing what you want, not by punishing her for not doing it.

- *Don't give up.* If your cat doesn't seem to be catching on to what you want, stop the session or work on something else. Come back to it later in the day and you may be surprised at what he remembers.

chapter ten

Dogs and Cats

When Nola and Darren decided to get married, they created a blended family. But it wasn't human stepsiblings who had to learn to get along. It was Nola's golden retriever, Chester, and Darren's Siamese cat, Ting, who found themselves in an unfamiliar situation. Unfortunately, Chester's reaction to Ting was to chase her. And while Ting would hiss and spit at Chester when trapped, she mostly just hid under the bed. The newlyweds felt they'd never see the time when all four family members could enjoy watching TV together.

Cats and dogs can get along. They can even become best friends. But they often need time to become accustomed to each other. Training—particularly for the dog—can be a real start on the path toward harmonious coexistence, or even friendship.

WHAT YOUR CAT IS TRYING TO TELL YOU

- *"Leave me alone!"* A cat can perceive attention from a dog as a threat.

- *"Don't make me hurt you."* Cats can and will use their claws on a dog's tender nose. Sometimes this can solve the problem, if it makes the dog change his threatening behavior.

- *"Give me an escape route."* Your cat needs a place, preferably someplace high, where she can get away from the dog when she feels threatened.

- *"Let me approach him on my terms."* Crating your dog or separating the two animals with a baby gate can put the ball in the cat's court and allow her to get comfortable with the dog at her own pace.

HOW TO SAY IT

- *Give your cat some control.* Use baby gates to stop the dog from chasing your cat into another room. One advantage of the gates is that the cat can go over (or under) them easily, while the dog stays confined. This allows the cat to approach the dog. If the dog tries to give chase, the gate stops him.

- *Give your cat a safe zone.* The room where the cat's litter box is should be out of bounds for your dog. She should be able to retreat there and use her litter box without fear of being chased or harassed. Put a baby gate on the door of this room, unless the mere sight of the dog is too stressful for the cat, in which case you should confine your cat to that safe room (with water and a scratching post and toys) until the two are more comfortable with each other.

- *Desensitize your cat to the dog.* Let your cat get more comfortable around the dog by crating your dog and letting your cat into the room with him. Give your cat treats for calm behavior around the dog. Slip some treats through the crate door to your dog, too, as long as he's being quiet.

- *Desensitize your dog to the cat.* Keep your dog on leash, perhaps tethered to your waist or even tethered to a piece of heavy furniture, and let the cat come as near as she'd like. Reward your dog for calm behavior. If your dog can't stay calm that close to the cat, then enlist a helper who can keep the cat farther away. Reward your dog and gradually bring the two closer together. Keep the sessions short at first. Don't push it and be sure to end on a high note.

- *Use Tellington TTouch.* Do gentle touches on each animal separately. Then, with a helper, work on both animals in the same room at the same time. This should help calm them and make them more comfortable with each other.

- *Provide high places for your cat.* Cats feel safer in elevated places. Be sure there's a safe place for your cat to jump out of the dog's reach.

- *Reward the dog for paying attention to you.* Practice rewarding your dog for looking at you. Then reward him like crazy when he looks at you in the presence of the cat. This teaches the dog that good things happen when he ignores the cat.

- *Try some flower essences.* Anaflora offers two flower essences that could help calm both animals as they're being introduced. Harmony aids in the introduction of a second animal to a home. Good Dog! helps relieves anxiety, uncertainty, inattentiveness, and resistance when a new behavior is being taught. (Anaflora suggests both human and dog take the essence.)

- *Visualize a peaceable kingdom.* Send mental images to both animals of the two peacefully coexisting, perhaps even snuggling.

HOW NOT TO SAY IT

- *Don't hold your cat when you introduce her to the dog.* She'll feel trapped and might hurt you in trying to scramble out of your arms. If you think she will run away and hide when she sees the dog, put her in her carrier so the two can check each other out safely. Keep your dog on his leash for this introduction.

- *Don't scream and holler.* It's easy to get hysterical if you're afraid your dog is going to hurt your cat. But by yelling, you're just adding to the problem. Stay calm and trust that the cat will be able to get out of the way.

- *Don't grab the cat.* If your cat's frightened, she's sure to scratch you. Don't try to scoop her up and hold her out of the dog's reach. Let her escape.

- *Don't give your dog the opportunity to chase when you're not home.* Keep the two animals separated when you're away so that your dog isn't rewarded (or your cat terrorized) by a good chase. Until you can trust them completely, bring the animals together only when you can supervise and reward calm behavior.

- *Don't punish your dog for cat chasing.* It's so rewarding to your dog to chase prey that your punishment would have to be very harsh and very well timed to deter him. Instead, motivate him by offering an even greater reward for not chasing the cat.

- *Don't rush it.* It may take a number of days (even weeks) of training before your dog can be trusted not to chase and your cat not to run. Be patient.

- *Don't mistake play for problem behavior.* It's possible your cat will invite a game of chase, which is okay. You want to avoid traumatizing your cat. But if your cat enjoys it and your dog is not out to harm her, let them play.

- Don't declaw your cat to reduce the chance of your dog's getting injured. The controversy surrounding declawing aside, if you remove your cat's claws, you remove her defenses. She'll feel more threatened by your dog and their relationship will deteriorate even further.

chapter eleven

Finding a Lost Cat

When Laura's husband accidentally let their indoor cat, Jake, out, he didn't even realize it. It wasn't until Laura came home, hours later, and Jake was nowhere to be found that they began to frantically search for their cat. Since Jake had been indoors since he was a kitten, they really feared for his safety.

Losing a cat is a huge nightmare for every loving pet owner. But for those who are dedicated to keeping their cats indoors, it is especially panic inducing. It can even happen to the most conscientious cat owner. The best way to recover a lost cat is to have considered the possibility ahead of time and be prepared for it. With preparation and persistence, the nightmare can have a happy ending.

WHAT YOUR CAT IS TRYING TO TELL YOU

- *"Find me!"* Depending on how far a cat has wandered, he may not be able to find his way home. If a Good Samaritan has taken him in, getting home might be completely out of his control.

- *"I'm just hiding."* Some cats can actually vanish in the house. There are lots of nooks and crannies, particularly in basements or closets, in which a cat can hide.

HOW TO SAY IT

- *Make a very descriptive sign.* Prepare some signs in advance (you can now purchase "Lost Cat" signs at pet-supply stores as well), so that all you have to do is add a current photograph, photocopy the sign, and put it up all over your neighborhood. Make sure the sign has all the pertinent information to help identify your cat (like markings, length of coat, whether the cat has been declawed, and any other identifying characteristics). Include a clear picture on the sign. And make sure all the information is easy to read, even by people in passing cars. As a precaution, put only your phone number, not your name or address, on your sign.

- *Keep current pictures of your cat.* As your cat ages, make sure you have a good picture of him that you can put on a sign. The photo should also clearly show any special markings. Keep your "Lost Cat" photo someplace where you can find it quickly, to save time searching through photos when you're frantic.

- *Consider a microchip.* ID tags are great because they're easily seen. But most cat collars are designed to come off easily (so the cat can't be hung up on the collar). A microchip injected between your cat's shoulder blades provides a permanent, unalterable form of identification, assuming your cat is taken somewhere (like a shelter or vet's office) with a microchip scanner. It's a fairly simple, innocuous procedure that, like any injection, might provide some temporary discomfort. Be sure that the chip number is linked to a database with your current information so that you—not the veterinarian or the shelter where you adopted the cat—are contacted when your cat is found. Keep that database updated when you move.

- *Go over the inside of your house with a fine-toothed comb.* If you didn't actually see your cat exit the house, perhaps she's lost inside. Grab a flashlight and go to the basement, the attic, and every other part of your house and look for hiding places. Look up—basements can have open spots in ductwork that cats can hide in. Open cupboards, closets, even the dishwasher and the laundry washer and dryer. Just because you don't hear your cat meowing doesn't mean that she's not in the house. She may be enjoying herself in her hiding place. Shaking a jar of treats or opening a can of cat food might bring her running.

- *Enlist your friends.* Get friends to help you canvass the neighborhood for your lost cat. They can look for your cat and also put up signs. Someone should stay home by the phone, in case your cat is found or comes home on her own. Your cell phone can become your best friend in times like these.

- *Go to your area shelters and look for your cat.* Fill out a lost-pet form. Then go back every day until your cat is found. Don't rely on phone calls to the shelters.

- *Contact area veterinary hospitals.* If your cat was injured when he was out loose (or even if he wasn't), he may have been taken to a veterinarian. Call the vets in the area and describe your cat. Or take your "Lost Cat" sign to all area vet hospitals.

- *Put an ad in the paper.* Most newspapers have a lost-and-found section in their classifieds. Place a "lost" ad. And don't forget to comb the "found" ads.

- *Distribute your sign far and wide.* Put it up at the grocery store; give it to all the delivery people you see in your neighborhood. Go door-to-door and give the flyer to your neighbors. Everyone should know that your cat is lost.

- *Use the Internet.* A number of websites (like www.missingpet.net, a volunteer group sponsored by the USDA Animal Care Office) help people find their lost pets. You can post a "Lost Cat" notice and look at notices for found animals. It might be a long shot, but no stone should be left unturned. See the appendix for more such Web sites.

- *Don't waste any time.* Get out there in your neighborhood and look for your cat before she's able to get very far. Be sure to take a carrier with you to put your cat in if you find her. Smelly treats might help lure her if she's frightened and needs extra incentive to come to you.

- *Don't sit back and wait for the phone to ring.* If your cat is lost, he needs you to take an active approach. Don't assume that shelters will call you.

- *Don't expect your cat to come home to you on her own.* She may not be able to if she's been injured or if she can't find her way. Perhaps someone found her and she's inside a house. Maybe she's trapped in a garage. Go out and try to find her.

- *Don't pay a reward before actually seeing your cat.* Sadly, con artists have been known to prey on people with lost animals, asking that money be sent before returning the cat. Also, don't go alone to meet anyone who says they've found your cat.

- *Don't forget to take down your signs when you find your cat.* If the signs remain in place, good-hearted people might go out of their way to find your cat. Your obsolete signs might detract from other "Lost Pet" signs that are current.

chapter twelve

Litter Boxes and Litter

Willow, an orange tabby, would confound her dad, Lyle, by perching on the edge of her litter box to eliminate rather than putting all four feet in it. Sometimes this meant she made a mess outside the box. Lyle had no idea why Willow would do such a thing—he'd always heard that cats trained themselves to use the litter box.

Cats are fastidious when it comes to their litter boxes. And they're also a little particular. Willow may not have liked the feel of the type of litter Lyle was using. To ensure that your cat uses her litter box each and every time, you need to select the litter based on your cat's preferences—not yours. And you must keep the litter clean. There's a vast array of litters available now, as well as a variety of litter boxes. Know your cat's litter-box preferences before making any decisions about new products.

WHAT YOUR CAT IS TRYING TO TELL YOU
- *"I need a clean litter box."* Just as humans don't like to use unflushed toilets, cats don't like to use dirty litter. It's up to you to keep it clean.

■ *"I have my own preferences."* Some cats like a covered litter box. Others hate them. Some like clay litter, others prefer pellets derived from newspaper. Some want a coarse litter, others want litter as soft as sand. Try to respect your cat's preferences when it comes to litter and box so that he'll respect your preference that he use the box.

HOW TO SAY IT

■ *Make sure that you have enough litter boxes.* The rule of thumb is one litter box per cat—plus one. If you have too few boxes, they might fill up faster than you can clean them, or your cat might have to stand in line to use one. You want to have fresh-smelling litter available to your cat whenever the urge to use it strikes. If your cat is older or infirm, have at least one litter box per floor of your house.

■ *Use the safest litter possible.* Remember that cats walk in the litter and then lick their paws. Whatever litter you use is likely to go into your cat. Clay clumping litters have been implicated—at least anecdotally—in intestinal blockages in cats. But that doesn't mean you have to avoid clumping litters altogether. There are at least three nonclay clumping litters on the market: the World's Best Cat Litter, made entirely of corn kernels, and S'Wheat Scoop and Heartland Wheat Litter, which, as their names imply, are made from wheat. Do your research before selecting a litter. See the appendix for sources of information.

■ *Be very careful with clumping litter and long-haired cats.* If the litter sticks to the hair on your cat's rear end, any moisture there could cause it to clump and stick, which would be very uncomfortable for your cat and even affect her ability to eliminate. If you have a long-haired cat, be sure to inspect that area after she uses clumping litter. If there's a problem, cut the hair short in the affected area and pay special attention during regular grooming.

■ *Expand the possibilities beyond clay.* If your cat doesn't like clay, there are a number of options these days. These include litter made from recycled paper (ECOFresh, Fibre Cycle, Yesterday's News, to name a few);

wheat (S'Wheat Scoop, Heartland Wheat Litter); corn kernels (World's Best Cat Litter) and corncobs (Field Fresh and Cobby Cat); and wood (Litter Love, Feline Pine). This list is by no means exhaustive.

■ *Look beyond the cat aisle.* Some material not marketed as kitty litter can be very effective. Wood pellets for pellet-burning stoves are used by some, as are alfalfa pellets, sold as rabbit food. Litter boxes might be found at crafts stores or in the storage-bin aisle in superstores.

■ *Recognize your declawed cat's special needs.* Cats who have had their claws surgically removed have especially sensitive paws (see the chapter on declawing). Most prefer softer litter, like the scoopable, clumping litters, which are quite fine. If your declawed cat is having litter box problems, try a softer litter.

■ *Consider a covered litter box.* Is your cat the shy type? He might prefer a covered box. Be sure he has clear access to the entry hole in the box. If your cat has asthma, however, a covered box might exacerbate the problem. One covered box, the Booda Box, has a built-in charcoal filter to help eliminate odors.

■ *Check out the brave new world of litter boxes.* High-tech litter boxes are now available: the Littermaid self-scooping box, for example, sends a rake across the litter ten minutes after the cat has used the box (it has censors that register the cat's comings and goings). It requires clumping litter and deposits the clumps in a covered compartment that has to be emptied periodically. The Litter Robot has a round compartment that the cat enters. Seven minutes after leaving the box, the compartment rotates, dumping clumps into a waste drawer. The LitterFree self-washing cat box lives up to its name by eliminating litter completely. More like a kitty toilet, it connects to your house's drainage system and uses washable, dust-free granules. Waste is automatically dissolved by water and drained, in a process that is repeated three times. Then a deodorizing solution is dispensed and drained. Finally, a dryer blows hot air on the reusable granules, which must be changed about every six months. Another relatively high-tech option is the KittySuite, which bills itself as "The World's Only

Completely Odorless Litter Box." It features a low-voltage fan that forces odor and airborne dust out of the house through a vent to a window or hole you put in the wall (like a dryer vent).

- *Look into another, less high-tech, but also potentially useful option: sifting litter boxes.* These boxes come in three parts. The top part, which has holes in its bottom, nestles into the bottom part (the third part, a bottom, is set aside for the next use). The litter goes over both. After the cat has used the box, you can lift out the top part and the litter falls through the holes, while the clumps stay in the top for disposal. After emptying the clumps from the top part, set it into the empty bottom part (which you've set aside), then pour the litter from the other bottom part over both.

- *Try a new device to make cleaning the box less unpleasant.* The Litter-Locker, a Diaper Genie–like device, sits next to the litter box. Scoop the box and deposit the clumps into the plastic-bag lined device, twist the wheel a half turn and the waste is sealed away, odor-free, for future disposal.

HOW NOT TO SAY IT

- *Don't use deodorizing litters.* If the litter box smells bad, clean it. Don't try to cover up the smell. Your cat's sense of smell is much stronger than yours, and deodorizers that smell pleasant to you might be an olfactory nightmare to your cat—and make the litter box less inviting.

- *Don't force a new litter on your cat.* If you want to switch litters, offer a second box to your cat with the new litter in it to see if she'll prefer it. If she doesn't, try putting a little of the new litter in with the old (reducing the amount if your cat refuses to use it). Once your cat is using a mixture, gradually add new litter each day, until your box is full of only new litter. If your cat balks at any point, go back to the proportions your cat will use and try again, this time adding less of the new litter.

- *Don't let price be your only guide.* If your cat happens to prefer the most inexpensive litter, that's terrific. But if the litter your cat will use consistently costs a little more, it's money well spent. Eliminating outside the box is not only stressful for your cat; it is hard on your relationship. Spring for litter he'll actually use. And keep it clean!

- *Don't put the litter box in an out-of-the-way place.* You want it to be conveniently located so that you can scoop it frequently (at least daily). You don't want it to be tucked away out of sight so that you forget about it until it starts stinking. Find a conveniently located place where your cat is comfortable and clean the box regularly so that odor isn't a problem for either of you.

chapter thirteen

Moving with Cats

Lauren and Bob were pleased to find a new house that matched both their taste and their budget. But they worried about how the stress of the move might affect their cats, Miney and Mo. They vowed to make the move as stress-free as possible for their cats, from the packing of the house to moving day itself to getting settled in their new home.

Moving can indeed be very stressful for cats—and why wouldn't it be? Moving is mighty stressful for humans (adults and kids) and cats aren't known for going with the flow. Some cats are more adaptable than others. But most tend to be resistant to change.

Moving is also fraught with potential dangers. But with good advance planning, a generous dose of paranoia, and the application of some common sense, you can make your move easier on your cat—and therefore easier on you.

WHAT YOUR CAT IS TRYING TO TELL YOU

- *"What's going on?"* Your cat is attuned to your stress level, which rises as the to-do list lengthens. The activity surrounding moving—the packing, throwing things away, the filled boxes piling up—does not escape your cat's notice.

- *"Am I coming with you?"* Your cat might worry that he's not going to be included on the adventure. A little reassurance can go a long way in helping alleviate that stress.

- *"What's this?"* Some cats may get curious and climb into the boxes while you're packing and pick through (or sleep on) the piles of discarded items.

- *"I don't want anything to do with this."* Your cat might go into hiding if there's too much activity. This could be especially difficult on moving day.

HOW TO SAY IT

- *Talk to him.* Tell your cat what's going on so the whole change in routine isn't a big mystery. He may or may not understand your words, but your intention will likely come through.

- *Keep her safe.* Safety should be a top priority. This means proper identification on your trip, even if your move is local. If it's long-distance, extra precautions should be taken (see the chapter on traveling with your cat). And it means, very importantly, that you eliminate any chance that your cat will escape on moving day.

- *Get him into a safe room.* Taking your cat away from the house on move-out and move-in day might be too stressful for him. A better option is to set up a safe room, one that you can empty before the movers get there. (A spare bathroom is a good choice.) Set the cat up with his litter box, his carrier, favorite toys, and his food and water (be sure to keep the food and water on the opposite side of the room from the litter box). Close the door, lock it, if you can, and put a skull and crossbones on the door. Make sure that it's absolutely clear to the movers and everyone else in the house that that door is not to be opened. Slip in to visit your cat periodically, to reassure him and give him needed attention. When the movers have cleared the rest of the house, put your cat in his carrier and take him (and his supplies) with you in the car. Then set up a safe room at your destination.

- *Treat the new house like it's a new home for your cat.* Start your cat out in a safe room, as recommended for introducing a cat into the household. Put her carrier into the room and open the carrier door so that she can emerge when she's comfortable. Keep the door closed until things settle down in the house. See the chapter on bringing your new cat home for more information on the introductions to the house. With any luck, this can go more quickly than when you first brought your cat home. But don't rush things. If your cat greets you at the door of his safe room, he's probably ready to explore —as long as the house has been cat-proofed.

- *Use some Feliway.* This simulated facial pheromone can have a calming effect on your cat. Stock up on the diffuser to use in your cat's safe rooms (on both ends of the move). You can also use Feliway spray to discourage your cat from marking should the move make him so inclined. As a preventive measure, spray it daily on prominent places that he might be inclined to mark with urine. See the chapter on spraying

- *Give her some flower essences.* The Bach flower remedy Rescue Remedy will help take the edge off your cat's stress. Don't wait until moving day—add it to her water as soon as you start packing. You might want to take some yourself. In addition, Anaflora makes a flower essence called Relocation that helps animals deal with the stress of a move.

- *Make sure your cat is comfortable in her carrier to minimize the stress of the actual relocation.* If feasible, some practice trips would serve a dual purpose: your cat would get to spend more time in the carrier and in the car, and it would alert you to any potential transport problems you might have to face on moving day.

- *Get a new vet right away.* If you're moving to a new city, make finding a new veterinarian a top priority. Stress can lead to physical problems in cats, and your cat may need you to take him to the vet sooner rather than later.

■ *Get back to your routine as soon as possible.* Returning to her normal schedule will help alleviate your cat's stress.

■ *Watch out for signs of physical problems in your cat.* Typical stress-induced problems include urinary tract and upper respiratory diseases. Keep an eye out for any change in your cat's litter-box habits, or runny eyes, sneezing, or other signs of physical problems. If you notice any symptoms, contact your vet.

■ *Make sure your cat is eating.* Cats who don't eat for several days are at risk of developing fatty liver disease. Keep a close eye on what your cat is eating. If the stress is prompting him to refuse to eat, pull out all the stops to make sure he ingests something each day. See the chapter on finicky eating for more information.

HOW NOT TO SAY IT

■ *Don't ignore your cat's needs.* There's so much going on during a move that it's easy to forget about one of the least demanding family members. But cats need reassurances and attention during stressful times.

■ *Don't let your cat roam in the new neighborhood.* If you have an indoor-outdoor cat, this move might be the perfect opportunity to transform her into an indoor-only cat (see the chapters on deciding whether to keep your cat indoors and on converting an outdoor cat into an indoor cat). If your cat simply is unable to remain happy indoors, despite your best efforts (see the chapter on keeping your cat happy indoors), at least keep her indoors for several weeks until the stress of the move dies down. Perhaps you could take her for a walk on leash to give her a tour of the new neighborhood.

■ *Don't leave stuff lying around that you don't want your cat to get to.* If your cat is stressed by the packing activities, he might start clawing or even spraying the piles. It's tempting to empty a closet and quit before you've finished packing it. But if you do, you might be asking for some cat-related damage.

■ *Don't put your cat's special things on the moving truck.* Her food and water bowls, litter box and litter, favorite toys and bed should go in the car with you so they can be unpacked right away. Put them into your cat's safe room before you let her out of the carrier in the new place.

■ *Don't blame the cat.* If your cat acts out during this stressful time, don't get too upset with him. His life's turning upside down and, unlike you, he has no control over it.

chapter fourteen

Nail Trimming

Trouble, a Maine Coon, lives up to his name whenever his owner, Marilyn, tries to trim his nails. When she grabs his paw and tries to extend his claw, Trouble turns into a terror, wriggling away and swiping at Marilyn with the same claws she's trying to trim.

Cat's claws are very important to them. They're their first line of defense against perceived enemies. And scratching on a scratching post (and not, with any luck, your couch) provides a great, muscle-toning stretch. It also helps your cat slough off the dead outer casing of his nails.

But scratching on the scratching post doesn't trim your cat's nails—that's something you have to do for him. Trimming nails is important—it minimizes the damage that your cat does to the furniture (or to you!). It also helps keep his claws from becoming snagged on the carpet or your sweater, since too-long nails can't retract all the way. Unfortunately, most cats aren't crazy about having their paws handled. But trimming nails doesn't have to be a battle. By trimming carefully and desensitizing your cat to the process, it can become a breeze.

- *"Those are my feet!"* Most cats don't like having their claws extended. Add to that a scary-looking implement touching their toes and it puts some cats into a panic.

- *"Get me out of here!"* Some cats can hurt you with their claws as they scramble to get away from the nail-trimming session.

- *"Hey, this isn't so bad."* If you desensitize your cat to the nail clippers, use lots of treats, and remain calm yourself, you can make the experience an easy one for your cat.

HOW TO SAY IT

- *Start early.* As soon as you get your cat, start acclimating him to the toenail clippers—and to having his feet handled. Touch his feet, his toes, all over his body, for that matter, keeping the mood upbeat and including food treats.

- *Do some groundwork.* Always touch your cat's paws when you're petting him. Massage your cat's toes while he's relaxed—this is well before you introduce the scary clipper—and extend the claws gently and lovingly. Regular massage can make nail trimming a breeze, since it accustoms your cat to enjoy having his whole body touched.

- *Desensitize your cat to the clippers.* Before you intend to actually clip, use a clicker to start getting your cat (no matter what her age) comfortable with the clippers. Have treats handy as you handle her feet. If she doesn't struggle, click and give her a treat. Extend her claws. More clicks and treats. Introduce the clippers. Let your cat see and sniff them. Then touch the clippers to your cat's foot, clicking for calm behavior. Keep the routine upbeat and brief, until she calmly accepts your actually cutting the nail. This may take several sessions.

- *Take it slow.* Don't rush the process. Slow, calm, and relaxed is the way to go. Work your way up to your cat calmly accepting the clippers near his feet. Only then should you actually trim the nail.

- *Use TTouches on your cat's paws to help her overcome her fear of nail trimming.* Do small circles on the paw, using only your fingertips. When she becomes comfortable with this, use the clippers themselves to do the circles.

- *Keep the clippers out in plain view.* If your cat gets spooked when you bring out the clippers, store them in plain sight—perhaps even near your cat's bowl—so that he develops a more blasé attitude about them.

- *Talk to your cat.* Keeping your voice soft and relaxed, let your cat know what you're doing and why. Be sure to tell her how good she's being.

- *Watch for the quick.* Before you ever start trimming, take a look at your cat's nails and you should see the pink quick running down the center. You don't want to trim into the quick; that would hurt your cat and turn future nail-trimming sessions into a struggle. Instead, cut the nail as short as you can, keeping your eye on the quick (and your clippers away from it). If your cat has dark nails so the quick doesn't show, cut off only the hooked part of the tip.

- *Clip regularly.* Try to make nail clipping a once-a-week routine. That way, your cat's nails will never get too long. If you make the sessions pleasant, it won't be a chore.

- *Use flour to stop bleeding.* If you do accidentally cut into the quick, dip the bleeding nail into a small dish of flour. It'll stop the bleeding without stinging.

- *Ask a vet or groomer for a lesson.* But be prepared: these professionals will make it look easy! Have them show you on one foot, then try replicating it on another so that the pro can tell you what you might be doing wrong.

HOW NOT TO SAY IT

- *Don't expect to clip all your cat's claws in one session.* Keep your sights low—and your session short—by clipping just one foot at a time at first. (Or even a single claw, if things aren't going well.) Even after you and your cat are used to the ritual, you might not be able to clip all four feet before your cat becomes impatient and wants you to stop.

- *Don't fumble while you're trimming your cat's claws.* After you've accustomed him to having his paws handled, plan your steps and motions for the actual clipping. Use smooth, gentle motions and talk to him with a soothing tone. This will help reassure your cat and give him less chance to wriggle away.

- *Don't punish your cat for struggling.* It's perfectly natural for your cat to want to avoid the procedure. Don't yell at her or forcibly restrain her. Instead, reward calm behavior and distract her with treats (using a helper, if possible). Remain patient.

- *Don't push it.* If you find yourself getting frustrated at your cat's protestations, put an end to the session and try again later. Try to end the session in an upbeat way. You don't want this procedure to damage your relationship.

- *Don't forget the dewclaws.* Cats have extra toenails on their front legs up near the dew pad. Think of them as kitty thumbs. Be sure to trim those as well.

chapter fifteen

Pet Sitters

Amy's work takes her away from home on two- or three-night trips fairly frequently. Her three cats seem to do well alone, but she worries that they're lonely or stressed in her absence. She wants to do the very best for her cats but doesn't know whether leaving them home (with a pet sitter coming in), taking them for care elsewhere, or taking them with her is the best option.

One of the reasons that people like having cats as pets is that they're less worrisome than dogs when left home while you travel. But cats are indeed social creatures and you shouldn't leave them entirely without care if you're taking any kind of extended trip. Getting someone to look in on them should be vital for your peace of mind, as well as for your cat's safety and comfort.

WHAT YOUR CAT IS TRYING TO TELL YOU

- *"I need a little company."* Your cat is used to having human companionship. If you are going on more than an overnight trip, your cat might start feeling lonely.

- *"Don't take me away from home!"* Most cats are better off staying in their home than being cared for in a boarding kennel, veterinarian's office, or friend's home.

- *"Take me with you."* Some cats are good travelers. For those cats, going with you on vacation might be the best bet.

HOW TO SAY IT

- *Get as much of your pet sitter's time as you can afford.* If you can find someone your cat likes to have stay in the house, that's the ideal. Otherwise, have someone come in as many times a day as possible.

- *Ask your sitter to do the things that you do.* Providing company as well as feeding and watering the cat and taking care of the litter box should be part of the pet sitter's duties. If your cat is willing, ask the sitter to provide some quality, interactive play time so that he gets mental and physical exercise. The sitter can also brush or comb your cat (as long as that's not stressful for the cat), stroke him, or just let him cuddle on her lap.

- *Even scaredy-cats need company.* If your cat isn't comfortable with strangers, let your pet sitter know that the cat might stay under the bed. But ask the sitter to talk with your cat, even if she can't see her. Reading aloud is a nice way to provide company without being intimidating.

- *Do your research.* If you don't have a trusted friend you can ask to look after your cat, ask your cat-loving friends whom they use. Or check the database of the National Association of Professional Pet Sitters. (See the appendix for contact information.) Don't forget to check references.

- *Interview the pet sitter over the phone or in person.* Have the pet sitter in to meet your cat and see the lay of the land before you take your trip. Listen to your gut: if the person doesn't feel right to you, don't use him or her.

- *Talk to your veterinarian.* If your cat has a chronic illness or needs injections, talk to your vet about hiring a vet tech to stay at your house. That would be less stressful than boarding the cat at the vet's office.

- *Swap pet care with friends.* If you have cat-loving friends, perhaps they can look in on your cats in your absence in exchange for your doing the same for them.

- *Leave written, not just oral, instructions for the pet sitter.* Try to cover all your bases, including emergency contact numbers as well as the veterinarian's address and phone number.

- *Leave an extra key with a trusted neighbor.* If there is a problem, and your pet sitter can't show up, at least someone will be able to get into your house.

- *Check up on them.* No matter what arrangements you make for your cat, don't be shy about calling the caregiver for updates. There may be small issues that the caregiver wouldn't want to phone you about but that you'd like the opportunity to weigh in on.

- *Leave behind something of yours.* Leave an unwashed T-shirt near your cat's bed so that your smell can keep her company. Or line a cardboard box with your unlaundered garment. She might enjoy lounging in the scent-filled box in your absence.

- *Consider a self-cleaning litter box.* If you don't want your pet sitter to have to scoop the litter box, or if you want to leave your cats overnight without any human company, a self-cleaning litter box, like the Littermaid, will ensure that they have a clean box to use. This will make your cats less stressed and will also reduce the chance you'll come home to find outside-the-box accidents.

- *Tell your cat what's going on.* Before you go on a trip, talk with your cat and tell him where you're going, why, and how long you'll be gone. That might take away the surprise of your absence and make your cat feel more comfortable. It certainly can't hurt.

- *Consider whether your cat might like to come along.* Some cats travel well and would rather come with you than be left home. See the chapter on traveling for tips.

- *Don't board your cat if you can help it.* It's stressful for cats to leave their home environments. And when cats are stressed, they're more likely to get ill. They're also more likely to pick up an infectious disease at a boarding facility than they would be at home. It's healthier for them to stay home.

- *Don't let your cat fend for herself.* Not only do cats need company, they need someone looking out for their health and safety. If you're going to be gone for more than one night, hire someone to come in and check on your cat, even if your cat spends the whole time the sitter is there under the bed. The cat's water needs to be refreshed, the litter box scooped, and the cat checked out for signs of stress or illness.

- *Don't let price necessarily be your guide.* This isn't a time to cut corners: price shouldn't be the number one factor in your decision about a pet sitter. Rather, reliability, kindness, interest, and references should be high on your list.

- *Don't sneak away.* If you try to pack while your cat's not around, or surreptitiously leave without telling your cat good-bye, you're denying her the opportunity to prepare. Don't take her by surprise, keep her in the loop.

chapter sixteen

Playing

Simon is such a couch potato that his owner, Marie, never even tries to play with him. All the big cat does is eat, groom himself, and sleep, it seems. He doesn't seem unhappy, but Marie wishes she saw him taking more joy in life.

Playing with your cat should be an essential part of your life together. Play serves several important purposes: It gives your cat exercise. It keeps your cat mentally stimulated. It taps into your cat's innate hunting and stalking skills. It's fun for your cat. And it provides the two of you with quality time together, which strengthens your bond. If you're not playing with your cat regularly, don't waste any time going to the pet-supply store for some fun toys. Or create some with supplies you have in the house!

WHAT YOUR CAT IS TRYING TO TELL YOU

- *"There's more to life than lying around."* Indoor cats, in particular, need the stimulation that play provides.

- *"I'm too fat."* Cats who get no exercise become fat cats. That's no healthier for your cat than it is for you.

- *"Let's spend some time together!"* While your cat can play by himself, it's more rewarding if you play with him, using interactive toys.

- *"I'm a mighty hunter."* Cat toys allow your cat to tap into his hunting skills.

HOW TO SAY IT

- *Buy toys you can play with together.* Wand toys, which typically have a wand or pole with a string attached, and something fun, like a feather, attached to the string, are great fun for both you and your cat. Wave the toy in the air, as well as along the floor, so your cat can pretend he's hunting both birds and mice. Be sure to let your cat catch the toy sometimes. You don't want it to turn into an exercise in frustration.

- *Get her toys she can play with on her own.* Toys that hang from doorways or knobs can make great solitary toys. Furry mice are very popular with most cats. She might like to play soccer with a Ping-Pong ball. Toys you can stuff with treats that fall out when your cat plays with them can be very stimulating. A new product called the Panic Mouse, which is battery operated, swings a "mouse" around at the end of a wire. A computer chip inside makes the movements unpredictable, and therefore more fun for the cat. If your cat spends a great deal of time alone, be sure she has toys she can play with. Rotate the toys to keep them fresh.

- *Try some homemade toys.* You don't have to spend a lot of money on toys. Many cats love to play in a paper bag. The plastic ring from the top of a milk jug is fun to bat around, as are pipe cleaners bent into various shapes. A ball made from a wadded piece of paper or a cork from a wine bottle makes a great retrieving toy. Cats can even have fun with a mini-marshmallow. Tissue paper is fun to hide under. If you have a fishing pole lying around, take off the hook and tie a toy to the end. Stuff an old sock with paper (spice it up with some catnip), tie off the end and drag it around on the floor for your cat to chase.

- *Be sure your toys are safe.* Don't give your cat anything sharp or anything inedible she can swallow. Rubber bands, yarn, dental floss . . . all are dangerous for cats.

- *Turn to play when behavior problems crop up.* Feline behaviorist and author Pam Johnson-Bennett often prescribes what she calls "play therapy" as a way to divert and refocus cats with behavior problems. "A cat engaged in unacceptable behavior can usually be distracted with an interactive toy," she writes in *Psycho Kitty: Understanding Your Cat's Crazy Behavior.*

- *Make play a part of your daily routine with your cat.* It's something both of you can look forward to.

HOW NOT TO SAY IT

- *Don't wake your cat up or interrupt his grooming for a play session.* Know your cat's rituals and pick a time to play when he's going to enjoy it most. Playing with him before mealtime will tap into his instincts of hunting for his meal before eating it. Playing before a midnight snack can help him sleep through the night—and allow you to do so.

- *Don't get into a rut.* Vary the toys you offer your cat. She can easily get bored with a single toy.

- *Don't give up.* If your cat doesn't seem to want to play with a new toy, put it away and try something else. It might just be a matter of getting the type of toy that catches his fancy. Or catching him when he's in the mood to play.

- *Don't let your cat play with string unsupervised.* Eating string can be very dangerous. So put your interactive toys away (and out of reach) when you're through with your play session.

chapter seventeen

Safety Issues

When Betty's cat, Poobah, suddenly started feeling ill one day, Betty couldn't imagine why. His diet hadn't changed at all and all household poisons were safely locked away—or so Betty thought. When she began mentally reviewing anything new to the household, she discovered the culprit: the new plant she'd brought in to liven up her house. Poobah had been chewing on a toxic plant and it sent him into acute kidney failure. Luckily, Betty got Poobah to the veterinarian in time and he made a full recovery.

There are many hidden hazards lurking around your house—and plenty outdoors as well. Take a look around and make sure that none of these unsafe items are within your cat's reach.

WHAT YOUR CAT IS TRYING TO TELL YOU

- *"I'm depending on you."* It's our world. Cats left to their own devices are pretty good about avoiding danger. But when we bring them into our homes, with our unique dangers, it's up to us to keep them safe.

- *"I'm a cat."* Cats do things that humans wouldn't dream of. They jump onto very high objects. They eat things that we would consider inedible.

Look at your home through your cat's eyes and remove any potential hazards.

HOW TO SAY IT

- *Keep your cat inside.* Probably the most important thing you can do for your cat's safety is to make him an indoor cat. See the chapter on deciding whether to keep your cat indoors for a discussion of the issues.

- *Supervise outdoor excursions.* If your cat is anxious to spend time outdoors, make sure she is safe. See the chapters on options for safe outdoor experiences and walking on leash.

- *Know your poisonous plants.* Most cats can't resist nibbling on plants. If you have a houseplant that your cat can chew, make sure it is not toxic. Many species of lilies, for instance, are extremely toxic to cats. See the appendix for information sources on toxic and safe plants. If you have any doubt, put the plant safely out of your cat's reach, or get it out of the house entirely. If your cat enjoys nibbling on plants, grow him some cat grass for that purpose. See the chapter on eating houseplants for more information on dealing with this habit.

- *Close your windows when you're not home.* An open window—even one covered by a screen—can pose a hazard to your cat. She could fall out and injure herself. Or she could simply escape the house. You might be surprised at how small a crack a kitten can squeeze through.

- *Play with your cat—but put away toys with string.* Interactive toys are important to help keep your cat physically and mentally fit. But those fishing-pole-type interactive toys can pose a danger if the cat plays with them unattended. Swallowing any type of string can damage your cat's gastrointestinal system. Put away these toys after every use.

- *Make sure your furniture is stable.* Cats are climbers. Don't risk a bookshelf tipping over with your cat on it. Wobbly furniture is an invitation to disaster.

- *Cover your electrical cords.* If you have an inquisitive cat who likes to chew on cords, you must eliminate access to them—or your cat could be electrocuted. Or he might pull something (like a lamp) down on top of him. Cover cords with aquarium tubing, tack cords to baseboards, or go to a baby store and buy a cord containment system meant to keep toddlers safe.

- *Kitty-proof your home.* Child safety latches help keep cabinet doors closed. If your cat likes to open cabinets, be sure to put childproof latches on the cabinets that contain household cleaners or any other poisons. Look for unsafe hiding places—like behind your refrigerator—which your cat could wedge herself into. When you find them, block access.

- *Close your toilet lid.* To prevent your kitten from a soggy surprise, keep the lid down. This also prevents your cat from drinking any cleaner-tinged water.

- *Consider a microchip.* If your cat goes outside—or tries to go outside—consider having a microchip implanted that will permanently identify him.

- *Be very alert while you're cooking.* If you're stirring a pot of something that smells good, your cat may try to jump onto the hot stove. Be ready to get her down—or discourage her when you see she's preparing to jump.

- *Keep your trash secure.* Put your trash can behind closed doors or take it out if it contains cooked bones or delicious-smelling plastic wrap. Both can damage your cat's system if eaten.

- *Think twice about what you leave in an uncovered wastebasket.* Seemingly innocuous items like dental floss, rubber bands, or discarded razor blades can become dangerous to cats if eaten. And you just never know what a cat will decide to eat.

- *Always use a carrier when transporting your cat.* Cats are consummate escape artists and they're great at hiding. Keep your cat safe in the car by putting him in a secure carrier. This prevents him from impeding your driving by running loose in the car and also keeps him safer in the event of a traffic accident.

- *Don't let drapery cords hang if your cat likes to play with them.* Your cat can get caught in the cord and be strangled while playing with it. Cut the cord short to keep it out of your cat's reach or fasten it to the wall.

- *Don't leave medications lying around.* An inquisitive cat can chew through a foil packet and eat a pill. Keep all medications out of your cat's reach, just as you would keep them away from children. Be sure to pick up any pills you drop on the floor.

- *Don't use automatic toilet bowl cleaners.* If your cat drinks out of the toilet, you don't want her drinking cleaning solution. Better yet, keep the toilet lid closed at all times.

- *Don't use lawn chemicals if your cat goes outside.* Eating chemically treated grass can be dangerous for your cat.

- *Don't use a dog collar on a cat.* Puppy collars are built to stay on a puppy—cat collars are made to slip off if they catch on something. If your cat goes outside, a collar and ID tag are important. But be sure it's an appropriate collar.

- *Don't let your cat get trapped.* Your cat can crawl under a recliner while the footrest is up and become trapped (or even crushed) when you lower it. He could wander into your dryer (or your dishwasher) and become trapped when the door is closed. Keep dryer doors closed and be aware of your cat's whereabouts when you are reclining in your easy chair. Keep closet and cupboard doors closed when not in use—but be sure there isn't a cat inside before you close the door.

- *Put out your candles.* Never leave a cat unattended near a lit candle. The flame could singe her fur—or even burn her skin. If you want to burn candles, buy holders (like deep votives or hurricane lamps) that encase the entire flame.

- *Don't smoke around your cat.* A study published in 2002 showed that cats who are exposed to tobacco smoke have a higher risk of lymphoma.

Breathing cigarette smoke is no better for your cat than it is for you. The difference is that you have a choice whether or not to smoke.

- *Forgo aromatherapy.* Many essential oils are toxic to cats when diffused in the air. That goes for simmering potpourri as well.

- *Don't allow your cat on a balcony.* Even if you're supervising her, a bird or insect could fly by and your distracted cat could take a dive.

chapter eighteen

Traveling with Your Cat

When Sarah and Pete moved from the Midwest to the East Coast, they naturally took their cats, Harry and Sally, with them. They were dreading the thousand-mile car journey, scared to death that something bad would happen to their precious cats. They worried they might not be able to find a hotel that would accept cats. And of course they worried that the trip would completely stress the cats out.

Cats don't tend to be the best travelers. Their canine counterparts tend to be more relaxed on the road (though of course there are exceptions). But you can take steps to make sure that your trip is as stress-free and safe for your cat as possible. Remember that when you are traveling with your cat, safety should be your most important consideration. Losing a cat in an unfamiliar locale would be unthinkably awful.

WHAT YOUR CAT IS TRYING TO TELL YOU

- *"Can't I just stay at home?"* Travel is frightening for many cats, particularly indoor cats whose horizons are very limited.

- *"I need my stuff."* If you travel with your cat, be sure to bring along the necessary equipment: carrier, litter box, scratching post or box, toys, and familiar food and water bowls.

HOW TO SAY IT

- *Properly (and prominently) identify your cat.* If your cat were to get lost while you were traveling, his regular collar tag with his home address and phone number wouldn't be much help. Create a special tag with your cell-phone number and an emergency number. Or use a paper key tag and a permanent marker to make a temporary tag with the phone number where you're staying each night. Or try the Jiffy Tag, a waterproof tag you write on with a pen, available for only fifty cents each from Animal Care Equipment & Services, Inc. (See appendix for contact info.)

- *Bring her own food and water.* Diarrhea can make traveling difficult for both you and your cat. Bring along a supply of your cat's regular food to minimize stomach upset. And if your cat is particularly sensitive, bring along some bottled water or tap water from home, since tap water can vary from place to place.

- *Use a cat carrier in the car.* It's absolutely essential that you contain your cat in the car. A loose cat could get under the brake pedal, creating a huge hazard. An uncontained cat is in real danger of injury in an accident. And she could become airborne in a collision and injure you. There are several types of carriers, some of which can be easily attached to your car's seat belt. Remember: it is as important for your cat to be protected in case of collision as it is for your human passengers.

- *Avoid air bags.* If your car is equipped with front-seat air bags, be sure your cat is in the backseat. Even if your cat is contained, he could be smothered by the air bag if the airholes in his carrier are blocked.

- *Be a considerate guest.* Always bring along your cat's litter box and use the type of litter she's used to. Scoop frequently to minimize odors and dispose of the scooped litter appropriately. If you allow your cat on the bed in a hotel room, bring along a sheet from home for her to lie on so that you don't leave behind cat hair and dander. If your cat complains loudly when left alone in a hotel room, don't leave her alone (order room service and eat in).

- *Bring along some Feliway.* This product, which simulates feline facial pheromones, is very soothing to cats. It comes in a spray or diffuser. Bringing along a diffuser would allow you to fill your hotel room with this calming, odorless product. You can also spray some in your cat's carrier to make it a more inviting place.

- *Cat-proof the room before letting your cat out of his carrier.* Remove anything that might be dangerous to your cat or that your cat might damage. Use the bathroom for an off-limits storage room for dangerous or breakable items, if necessary. Make sure all windows are closed.

- *Consider traveling with a pet tent.* SturdiProducts, which makes the SturdiBag carrier, also sells a collapsible Pet Tent, which can provide a secure, roomy place for your cat to relax inside your hotel room. The nylon-and-mesh tent pops open to 36×36×24 inches and collapses to fit into a 9-inch storage bag. See the appendix for purchasing information.

- *Get a travel (or disposable) litter box.* Some litter is sold in a cardboard box that you can use on trips. Rather than scooping or emptying it, you can just toss it away. SturdiProducts makes a reusable leak-proof nylon litter box that fits inside some of its carriers.

- *Try some calming flower essences.* Rescue Remedy can help calm your cat down if he's anxious about traveling.

- *Do ear touches for carsick cats.* If your cat throws up in the car, try doing some TTouch ear touches. It should help with nausea.

HOW NOT TO SAY IT

- *Don't leave your cat alone in the car.* In warm weather, the car can heat up to deadly temperatures within minutes. If you have to stop at a rest area on a warm day, blast the car's air-conditioning as you approach the

Flying with Your Cat

If at all possible, fly your cat with you in the cabin, safely tucked under the seat in front of you. Don't check her as baggage. Flying in the cargo hold would be very stressful—and potentially dangerous—for your cat.

When flying with your cat, keep the following things in mind:

- Your cat will need a reservation—and you'll probably have to pay a fee for her to travel.

- You'll need an airline-approved carrier that will fit under the seat in front of you.

- Your cat will have to pass through security, which means she will probably have to come out of her carrier so it can be X-rayed. Keep a collar, with ID tags, on your cat for the trip. Put a harness on her, too, so that you can clip a leash on it before taking her out of the carrier at the security checkpoint (or just leave a lightweight leash attached to the harness for the whole flight).

- The airline might have regulations about proof of vaccinations—be sure and check in advance so that you have the proper paperwork.

- You should prominently mark your carrier LIVE ANIMAL, even though you plan to be with the carrier at all times. Soft-sided carriers can look like ordinary carry-on bags; should you and your cat somehow become separated, you'll want people to know there's a cat inside.

stop. Then dash in and use the facilities before letting your cat out of her carrier to use the litter box in the car or resuming the trip. Always park in the shade if possible and minimize the time your cat is left alone in the car. Alternatively, take your cat (in his carrier) into the rest room with you. Be nonchalant about it to avoid any protest from non–cat lovers.

- *Don't let your cat loose.* Even if your cat is an outdoor cat, don't risk letting her outside in an unfamiliar place. Leash-train her before you take your trip so that you have a safety net when putting her in and out of her carrier, and be sure she can't wriggle out of her harness. Resist the temptation to let her out to stretch her legs while you're on the road. You don't want to lose your cat at a roadside rest stop. Instead, use interactive toys to exercise your cat inside once you get to your destination.

- *Don't sedate your cat.* If you're flying your cat, it might be tempting to sedate him. But sedation can affect your cat's respiration (particularly if he's flat-nosed), which can become an issue at high altitudes. Instead, try calming flower essences, like Rescue Remedy.

- *Don't assume everybody likes your cat.* You may have the sweetest cat in the world. But some people just dislike—or even fear—cats. Don't foist your cat on others while you're traveling.

part two

Keeping Your Cat Healthy

We're seeing a shift in thinking by many progressive cat owners about their cat's health care. People have begun questioning the need for routine annual revaccination, for example. More cat owners are preparing their cats' food at home, or at least scrutinizing the labels of the commercial food for better ingredients. Holistic veterinarians are becoming increasingly popular as people seek ways to keep their cats healthy or look for alternative ways to treat serious illness.

The best way you can help your cat's health is to listen to him. If he tells you that he isn't feeling well, pay attention, even if the clues are very subtle. Build a relationship with your veterinarian so that you're not embarrassed to call and say that something's just not right. Look for a vet who listens to every comment you make about changes in your cat. You know your cat better than anyone, and your observations are the basis upon which your veterinarian makes treatment recommendations.

Taking good care of your cat's health is much like taking care of your own. If your cat becomes ill, you should research the illness so that you can ask educated questions of your veterinarian. Get a second opinion, if you think it's warranted. Apply critical thinking when your vet makes recommendations, rather than accepting them automatically. Your cat depends upon you to be his health care advocate.

chapter nineteen

Declawing

Damon's cat, Seamus, was ruining his house. He'd come home to find his curtains in tatters. The condition of his couch was deteriorating by the day. Worse yet, when Seamus would play, he'd leave painful scratches on Damon's hands. It was starting to affect how Damon felt about his cat, whom he really wanted to love. He decided that maybe the only answer was to declaw Seamus.

Declawing is seldom the only answer, though as a true last resort—when all other options have been exhausted—it can be better than rehoming or euthanasia.

Before you make a decision to declaw your destructive cat, take the time to learn about the complex surgical procedure. And be sure to try nonsurgical options to tackle the clawing problem.

WHAT YOUR CAT IS TRYING TO TELL YOU

- *"My claws are important to me."* Claws are an important part of your cat's survival mechanism. To remove them is to remove one of his most important tools.

- *"Don't amputate my toes."* As awful as it would seem to have your fingernails removed, it's even harder on a cat to have her claws removed. Because claws retract, the procedure actually requires amputation of the last portion of each digit.

- *"I need a place to scratch."* If your cat's scratching is destructive, providing an appropriate place for him to scratch (and removing the temptation of his favorite scratching objects) can take care of the problem.

HOW TO SAY IT

- *Learn what the procedure entails.* In a nutshell, declawing is major surgery, involving the surgical amputation of the last joint of each toe, including the bone (essentially ten amputations if only the front paws are done). The risks and ramifications of the procedure include:
  - ❏ A reaction to the general anesthesia
  - ❏ A painful recovery
  - ❏ Bleeding after the bandages are removed
  - ❏ Possible abnormal regrowth of the claws
  - ❏ Weakened leg, back, and shoulder muscles from the disruption of natural stretching and clawing rituals
  - ❏ Potential injury from the inability to defend herself with her claws
  - ❏ Irritability and defensiveness
  - ❏ Litter-box problems from sensitive paws

- *Seek out other remedies first.* There are many ways to address the problem of furniture scratching (see the chapter on clawing the furniture) as well as scratching people (see the chapter on biting and scratching). With some effort, you can teach your cat to use his claws appropriately and declawing shouldn't be necessary.

- *Consider the emotional ramifications.* "Because they are defenseless, declawed cats live in a constant state of stress," writes Anitra Frazier in *The New Natural Cat.* In addition to being unhappy, stressed cats are more prone to disease.

- *Understand that declawing is extremely controversial.* It is illegal in Australia, Germany, and other countries. The British Veterinary Association's policy states, "The removal of claws in cats is undesirable and should only be carried out in extreme circumstances when the alternative is euthanasia." The city of West Hollywood, California, has banned the declawing of cats. Some veterinarians in the United States refuse to declaw. The Humane Society of the United States opposes it. The Cat Fanciers' Association in the United States officially disapproves of it and does not allow declawed cats in the show ring.

- *Think about covering the nails instead.* Soft Paws® are plastic tips, which blunt the claws, that are glued over each claw. They must be reapplied every few weeks (or more often if your cat manages to chew them off). Some cats require anesthesia to have the Soft Paws applied, but if your cat can tolerate your applying them at home, Soft Paws is a more humane alternative to declawing. Providing a place for your cat to scratch and encouraging her to use it is an even more humane solution.

- *If you must declaw, use the most modern methods.* Laser surgery can provide a less painful recovery. If declawing is your only option, see if you can find a surgeon experienced in laser surgery.

HOW NOT TO SAY IT

- *Don't let your declawed cat outside.* If you decide to have the procedure done—or if it's been done in the past—keep your declawed cat indoors. If he goes outside, he's defenseless. Even his climbing might be inhibited. Declawed cats should remain in the house. Period.

- *Don't cut the tendons.* An alternate surgical procedure for keeping cats from scratching is to cut the tendons that allow the cat to extend his claws. Don't consider this a more humane option. While potentially less painful, it is also debilitating to cats. It can lead to joint fusion or arthritis. The claws will grow without the benefit of the cat's scratching to shed the outer layers. Your cat will require a regular manicure; without it, his claws could grow around and become embedded in his pads. And the emotional effects of not being able to extend the claws could be profound.

■ *Don't inhibit your cat's communication by declawing.* Cats use their claws as a form of communication. Their kneading represents contentment. A gentle touch with claws sheathed can be a show of affection. Claws extended, without scratching, can be a warning. A swipe with exposed claws toward a dog sends a clear message that most dogs will listen to.

chapter twenty

Diet: How to Feed

B rad's cat, Gidget, doesn't always want to eat her meals. Brad's tried changing what he feeds, where he feeds Gidget, the time of day he feeds, and even what type of bowl he uses. Sometimes Gidget will eat, other times she just walks away. Occasionally, she'll stare nervously at her food.

Cats are very particular about eating. In the wild, they're solitary hunters and eaters. They're very attuned to the threat of competitors coming into their territory. They're also creatures of habit, so changing their feeding routine can be upsetting enough to make them not want to eat at all. It's important that a cat eats—fasting can actually cause illness—so establishing good eating practices and being consistent with them will help your cat stay on an even keel.

WHAT YOUR CAT IS TRYING TO TELL YOU

- *"Keep it natural."* Devise your feeding plan around a wild cat's natural eating habits.

- *"I need security."* Feed your cat in location that allows her to feel safe. If she's worrying that a dog or another cat will steal her food, meals turn into a source of anxiety, not enjoyment.

- *"I need consistency."* Don't constantly change how you feed your cat. Give him the stability of a routine place and time to eat.

HOW TO SAY IT

- *Feed a high-quality diet.* Cats require meat (as well as other sources of nutrients). Offer your cat the best-quality food you can. See the chapter on what to feed your cat for more information on what constitutes high-quality food.

- *Feed at regular intervals.* Feed your cat two or three meals a day and take up the food after a half hour if she hasn't finished. This replicates the natural way that cats eat—by immediately devouring the prey that they've hunted. Leaving food out all day for your cat isn't optimal (see following page).

- *Give your cat some privacy.* If necessary, feed him on the counter or even the top of the refrigerator (if he's nimble) to keep him from feeling threatened by other animals or people in the household.

- *Keep your cat's dishes clean.* Wash her bowl after she eats or put it in the dishwasher for washing later. Such simple hygienic practices, that we take for granted for ourselves, should also be applied to our pets.

- *Adjust how much you feed based on your cat's weight.* Ask your veterinarian what your cat's ideal weight is and use a bathroom scale to keep track of it (weigh yourself holding your cat and subtract your weight). If your cat is gaining weight, cut back on his food. If he is losing weight, increase it. If he continues to lose weight, see your vet—unexplained weight loss can be a sign of disease.

HOW NOT TO SAY IT

- *Don't feed near the litter box.* Cats naturally avoid eliminating near their eating area. In the wild, urine smells attract predators—and a cat wants to keep predators away from his nest. A food bowl near the litter box may force your cat to eliminate elsewhere.

- *Don't feed in a high-traffic area.* Your cat should be fed where she's comfortable, and that's usually not in the middle of a traffic pattern in your house. Elevate her bowl off the kitchen floor and onto the counter or other safe place. That way she doesn't have to look over her shoulder nervously while she's eating. Feed her in the same place every meal; cats love the stability of routine.

- *Don't free-feed.* Allowing your cat access to food at all times might be easier for you. And your cat might think it's swell. But cats in the wild don't nibble all day. They hunt and they eat a meal of what they've just hunted. Spacing your cat's meals allows his body to digest properly and work on keeping itself healthy. Anitra Frazier writes in *The New Natural Cat* that the smell of food triggers the brain to prepare the body for digestion. So if food is sitting around where your cat can smell it all day, his body is constantly preparing for digestion—and blood is being sent to the stomach rather than to the other organs. This is not healthy. Another reason not to free-feed, according to Frazier, is that the smell of the food prompts the cat's body to make his urine more alkaline, which contributes to lower urinary tract problems (see the chapter on urinary tract problems).

- *Don't overfeed.* If your cat is fat, she's eating too much, and not getting enough exercise. Either decrease the amount you feed your cat or increase her exercise (daily play sessions with an interactive toy will do the trick). Obesity is no less healthy in cats than it is in humans. Do your cat a favor and keep her in good shape.

- *Don't fast your cat.* If your cat—especially an overweight cat—is fasted (or fasts himself) he risks developing fatty liver disease, which is potentially fatal. In this disease, also called hepatic lipidosis, the liver accumulates fat as a result of the body's using stored fat for energy rather than getting energy from food. Liver function decreases, the cat feels worse and doesn't want to eat, and the cycle continues as liver function worsens. Fatty liver disease, which can be fatal, can develop if a cat stops eating for as little as two days.

- *Don't use plastic bowls.* Some cats have a reaction to plastic. Plastic bowls are porous and retain bacteria, and they're hard to get really clean and odor-free. A better option is stainless steel or glass.

chapter twenty-one

Diet: What to Feed

Tiffany's cat, Homer, has crystals in his urine. She keeps a close eye on his litter-box habits and takes him to the vet when she sees him straining to urinate. The vet has suggested special, prescription-only food for Homer, but Tiffany hesitates to spend the extra money. What she doesn't realize is that by spending some extra money and time on her cat's diet, she can help Homer lick his crystal problem and become healthier overall. Prescription food may not be the best solution, however.

That old axiom "You are what you eat" applies to cats as much as it applies to humans. Good nutrition is the cornerstone of good health. When cats suffer from poor nutrition (or from food allergies) it often shows up in a dull, flaky coat, itchiness, gastrointestinal upset, urinary tract problems, and general ill health. And, sometimes, poor nutrition is the culprit when a cat has behavior problems.

Commercial cat foods all purport to be "complete and balanced," yet there is a huge disparity among brands. Being aware of cat-food ingredients and buying the best cat food you can afford, or even preparing food for your cat yourself, can help keep your cat in tip-top shape.

- *"This food isn't giving me what I need."* If your cat isn't vibrant or suffers from low-grade chronic illness, perhaps you need to switch to a higher-quality food.

- *"My food makes me feel bad."* If your cat is sensitive or allergic to a component of his food—be it a food ingredient or an additive—his food can actually make him sick.

- *"How about some variety?"* For years, veterinarians and pet-food manufacturers insisted that pets don't need variety in their diet and that it was best to stick to one brand of food. How would you like to eat nothing but one brand of cereal or one flavor of canned soup every single day? Holistic vets advocate lots of variety in a cat's diet. Cats crave variety—and their bodies need it, too. Many people think that cats are overly finicky—perhaps it's just their way of asking for more variety. Sticking to one kind of food can make cats even more finicky.

- *"Give me some meat!"* Cats cannot survive without meat in their diets, so don't try to make him a vegetarian.

HOW TO SAY IT

- *Buy the best you can afford.* Higher-quality ingredients cost more. But high prices don't necessary equate with high quality. A lot of money can go into marketing and packaging rather than ingredients.

- *Learn to read a label.* If you're serving your cat commercial cat food, know what's in it. Look for specific meats (like beef, poultry, or lamb) in the first three ingredients. Avoid food with by-products, especially those whose only meat ingredient is by-product, as well as "meat" or "animal" meals. Minimize grains—they're an inexpensive source of protein, but cats aren't built to process them well. (Feeding wet food over dry is one way to minimize grains.) Avoid any food with sugar and flavoring added and with artificial preservatives. See the appendix for further reading on pet-food ingredients.

- *Consider a home-prepared diet.* Some cat owners choose to feed a more natural diet of raw meat, bones, organs, and vegetables or to cook up a stew for their cat. Generally speaking, the idea is to replicate the cat's natural prey—mice or birds—with vegetables supplying the fiber that fur or feathers would naturally provide. A few companies provide ready-made raw (frozen) food for cats. See the appendix for details.

- *Do your research.* If you decide that you'd like to prepare your cat's food yourself, don't just wade into it without informing yourself on cat nutrition. For example, while meat is essential, a meat-only diet is not healthy for cats, because it lacks certain minerals, like calcium. Vegetables must be processed (put through a food processor or cooked) for your cat to digest them. Learn the basics of feline nutrition so that you're providing nutrition that is balanced over time.

- *Feed a variety of foods.* Whether you feed a home-prepared or high-quality commercial diet, give your cat a good variety of meat sources and other ingredients. It'll help keep her from getting finicky and will help supply all the nutrients she needs for optimal health.

- *Try some bones.* Raw bones can be very nutritious for your cat. Most cats won't crunch down on a chicken neck (though some will), but you can grind raw, meaty bones.

- *Think about whole foods.* Some especially devoted cat owners purchase whole prey for their cats to eat. Baby mice, chicks, quail are all species-appropriate foods for your cat. These foods can be purchased from snake-food suppliers. See the appendix for more information.

- *Give her a digestive enzyme.* A digestive enzyme like Prozyme, which is made for dogs and cats, or one made for humans available at a health food store, can help your cat digest her food better.

- *Transition your cat slowly.* If you are changing your cat's food, try adding a bit of the new food to the old and slowly switch your cat over. This will help avoid digestive upset and can make the transition easier on your finicky cat.

- *Watch out for preservatives.* Most holistic vets feel that chemical preservatives found in pet food, like BHA, BHT, and ethoxyquin, are to be avoided. Look for naturally preserved foods.

- *Provide abundant and clean water.* Filtered water is best. Water intake is important, particularly if your cat eats dry food. Ample fresh water should be available at all times. Talk to your veterinarian if your cat's water intake changes noticeably.

HOW NOT TO SAY IT

- *Don't feed dry food exclusively.* It's less appropriate for cats, whose natural diet is meat, not grains. It's hard on cats' kidneys. And it's especially dangerous for cats with urinary tract problems (because of the low moisture content). If your cat insists upon eating dry, make sure that at least half his food is either canned or home prepared.

- *Don't try to turn your cat into a vegetarian.* Even if you yourself are the picture of health as a vegetarian, don't impose it on your cat. Cats are obligate carnivores: they require meat in order to live. A cat who is fed a vegetarian diet will live a substandard life.

- *Don't buy the cheapest food for your cat.* Inexpensive food is made from inexpensive ingredients. In general, inexpensive filler ingredients, like brewer's rice (the waste product of commercial beer brewing), don't provide your cat with good nutrition.

- *Don't feed tuna on a regular basis.* Cats love tuna. But they also can become addicted to it—and it's not a healthy food for them. The mercury in tuna is cause for concern, and canned tuna is high in polyunsaturated fats, which cats don't metabolize well. The routine feeding of tuna can lead to vitamin-E deficiency, which can cause a painful inflammatory condition called steatitis (also known as yellow fat disease).

- *Don't feed a homemade diet without doing research first.* If you decide to take your cat's nutrition into your own hands, make sure you know what you're doing. Some vets will tell you that you can't possibly provide a balanced diet. But if you have kids, you probably manage to feed them properly. Just do some research. Read books, talk to a veterinarian open to home-prepared diets, talk to others who are doing it. Internet mailing lists are a great way to interact with experienced home feeders. Your cat depends on you to provide him with good nutrition, so make the effort to know what you're doing first. See the appendix for information resources on home-prepared diets.

- *Don't starve your cat into eating a new food.* Cats can become ill if they don't eat on a daily basis. If your cat isn't accepting the new food, give her some of the old so that she goes to sleep with food in her belly.

- *Don't feed your cat a diet of dog food.* Dogs and cats have different nutritional requirements. A diet exclusively of dog food is not healthy for your cat. (The reverse is true as well.) Be sure to provide a species-appropriate diet.

chapter twenty-two

Euthanasia

Dara knew that her sixteen-year-old Persian, Alexander, was dying. His kidneys were failing, his appetite was nonexistent, and he was extremely lethargic. The thought of having her precious kitty put to sleep was more than she could bear.

Contemplating the death of your cat is very painful. But thinking about it in advance can help you make decisions before you're faced with a crisis. Euthanasia can be a last gift you can give your cat. Ideally, the procedure is planned and peaceful. Understanding what your options are for euthanasia, and being in tune with your pet so that you know when the decision is right, can help you make this time less painful.

WHAT YOUR CAT IS TRYING TO TELL YOU

- *"I love you, but life is no longer good."* If your cat's illness results in pain, inability to walk easily, or loss of bowel and urinary control, these might be signs that quality of life has deteriorated to the point where euthanasia is the most humane solution.

- *"Please let me go."* If your cat is terminally ill and his quality of life has diminished, he'll try to tell you that it's his time to go. Stay connected with him and look for clues in his eyes.

- *"I'd like to die at home."* If your cat is stressed by car trips or visits to the veterinarian's office, talk with your vet about the possibility of coming to your house to administer euthanasia. If that's not possible, look for a house-call vet in your community who might be able to help.

HOW TO SAY IT

- *Talk to your cat.* If he's very ill or seriously injured, look into his eyes and ask him to tell you if he's ready to go and if he needs help. Tell him that if he feels it's time to go on his own, that's okay, too. Sometimes cats will hang on for our sake.

- *Listen to your cat.* Look for indications on her part that death would be a mercy. While each individual is different, pain, unwillingness to eat, difficulty breathing, and undignified living conditions may be signs that euthanasia would be welcome.

- *Try to be there for your cat.* As painful as it may be, being present during your cat's euthanasia can provide comfort for both of you. Some people regret being absent during their pet's final moments. You may be surprised at how peaceful the process is.

- *Ask your vet for sedation for your cat.* The lethal solution that your vet will give your cat to cause death (an overdose of anesthesia) must be administered intravenously. Because it can be difficult for your vet to find a vein—and the search for the vein can be extremely stressful for both you and your cat—ask the vet to sedate your cat with a shot under his skin first. That way, your cat will go into a deep sleep, free of pain, during which you can say your last good-byes. He won't be bothered as your vet looks for a vein.

- *Be prepared for some natural reactions.* Your cat may gasp before dying—a purely physical reaction that doesn't indicate pain or distress. She will also probably empty her bowels and bladder. Again, this is perfectly natural.

- *Discuss euthanasia options with your vet in advance.* Find out if she's willing to do the procedure at your home, how much advance notice she needs, and whether there's a particular time of day that works best for her (whether you have the procedure done in the office or at home).

- *Know what you'll do with the remains.* You may wish to bury your cat's body. Or you may want to have her cremated. Ask at the vet's office whether they offer private cremation and whether you can get the ashes back. Whatever you choose, it's best to think about it in advance so you're not making a hasty decision that you can't take back.

- *Give yourself permission to grieve.* You're losing a family member. Even if society doesn't understand the depth of your feelings for your cat, you should acknowledge them. So take the time to grieve and to remember the good life you had together. See if you can take some time off from work to grieve privately.

- *Seek help in dealing with your loss.* Pet-loss support groups are on the rise. Call your veterinarian or local humane society to see if you can get help from a local organization. See the appendix for more information.

HOW NOT TO SAY IT

- *Don't keep your cat alive just because you can't bear to live without him.* If you know in your heart that he needs help in dying, let him go, for his sake, if not yours.

- *Don't assume that a natural death is necessarily better.* It might be preferable for your cat to go on her own, but if she is suffering, exercise the humane alternative that people have for their pets. It can be the last favor you do for your cat.

- *Don't be pressured into euthanasia.* If there's a disagreement among family members about whether it's time to euthanize a cat, try to reach a mutual decision so that resentment doesn't linger. Look to your cat for clues.

chapter twenty-three

Giving Oral Medications

When Sarah brought her cat, Loki, to the vet, he had good news and bad news. The good news was that he'd found a cause for Loki's gradual weight loss—an overactive thyroid gland—and that the condition was treatable. The bad news was that Sarah would have to give her cat a pill every day for the rest of his life. The prospect made her quake in her boots.

Giving medication to cats isn't necessarily difficult—but for some cats it can be a frightening prospect. There are some less aggressive options to try before forcing a pill down your cat's throat. But even if you have to do this, some simple techniques can make the procedure less onerous for both you and your cat.

WHAT YOUR CAT IS TRYING TO TELL YOU

- *"You're trying to poison me—and I'm not falling for it."* Many cats can't be tricked by pills that are hidden in a tasty tidbit.

- *"Are you crazy?"* Cats hate to be forced to do anything. Holding their mouth open and sticking a pill down their throat must top their list of simply insane things that humans do to them.

- *"I trust you."* When your cat allows you to give him medication without a great struggle, he's telling you that he knows that your most mysterious behavior is still for his benefit. Pat yourself on the back.

HOW TO SAY IT

- *Hide the pill.* The least stressful way to get your cat to take a pill involves a little subterfuge. Put it in a delicious substance (or split it and give half at a time). Cream cheese can work (salmon flavored is particularly tempting), as can wet cat food, baby food, canned fish, or any other tasty, sticky substance. Tell your cat you have an important treat, put the pill wrapped in its disguise on your fingertip, and let him lick it off. When your veterinarian gives you the pills, check to make sure that putting the pill in food won't hamper its effectiveness.

- *Grind the pill.* Buy an inexpensive pill grinder to turn tablets into powder. Assuming that the powder doesn't taste too bad, you can mix this in with a small amount of food for your kitty to eat. No suspicious lumps in the food. Similarly, you can empty capsules into food.

- *Try a pill shooter.* Pet-supply stores sell small plastic "guns" to help pill-unwilling animals. The pill sticks to the end of the gun, allowing you to painlessly shoot the pill into the back of your cat's mouth.

- *Get better-tasting medication.* Ask your vet if he or she would be willing to work with a compounding pharmacist to come up with a medication specifically designed to be palatable to your cat. (Compounding pharmacists are old-fashioned pharmacists who create custom medications.) Many will make liver-flavored chewable pills, for example, or liquid medications in a fish-flavored suspension. If you can turn medicine into a treat, you and your cat will both benefit!

- *If your cat simply won't view a pill as a treat, you'll have to pop it in manually.* Gently tilt her head up just a little, pry open her jaw, and use one finger to drop the pill in the back of her throat, past the hump in her tongue. Be sure the fingernail on the pill-pushing finger is very short, or you risk scratching the roof of her mouth. You can stroke her throat, but don't hold her mouth closed. Cats swallow with their mouths slightly open. Watch for her to lick her lips or nose—that's a sign she's swallowed.

- *If your cat squirms a lot, wrap him in a towel, with just his head sticking out.* It'll keep him from scratching you during the procedure. Think of it as his swaddling clothes. This should make him feel secure while protecting you from injury. You might need an assistant to help you keep the swaddled cat in place while you pill him.

- *Give her liquid.* Liquid medications may seem like they'd be easier to administer than pills, but that's an individual matter. If your vet gives you a liquid, first try putting it into a small amount of food (after making sure that it's okay to give the medication with food). If she doesn't go for that, use the same procedure as for a pill, except squirt in the liquid into her cheek pouch a little at a time. You can use a plastic eyedropper (a glass one might break if bitten) or a syringe without a needle.

- *Talk to him.* No matter what method you use, tell your cat what's up, using soothing tones. Don't grab him and take him by surprise. Your loving intention will come through in your tone and perhaps even your words. You want him to understand that you're doing it for his own good.

- *Reward her.* Once the medication is in your cat, reward her with a treat or special petting session. The food treat has the double benefit of making her swallow more—minimizing the chance that you'll find a spit-out pill on the floor hours later.

HOW NOT TO SAY IT

- *Don't fumble.* Try to make pill giving as clean and calm a procedure as you can. No big deal, open the mouth, pop in the pill, watch for the swallow. If you turn it into a drama, your cat may never get used to it.

- *Don't chase your cat around in order to grab him and pill him.* Make the procedure as low-stress as possible by gently handling your cat and soothingly talking with him about what's about to happen.

- *Don't lose your temper.* It can be very frustrating when your cat struggles while you're trying to do something for her own good. But remember that she's simply being a cat. Losing your temper will only make it worse.

- *Don't hold your cat's mouth shut after you give him a pill.* He needs his mouth to be slightly open in order to swallow with ease.

chapter twenty-four

Going to the Veterinarian

Sherry's calico cat, Millie, is the nervous type, and going to the veterinarian's office makes her absolutely miserable. She tries to hide under the exam table and scrambles out of Sherry's arms when she tries to hold her. The veterinarian is a little nervous that Millie will bite or scratch her. The whole experience is so nerve-racking that Sherry dreads taking Millie to the doctor.

Going to the veterinarian is just one of those things that cats have to endure sometimes. If you avoid going because your cat gets so worked up, you might be putting her health in danger. Don't delay taking your cat to the veterinarian if something is wrong. And don't skip the annual wellness exams. Rather, work on making the trip to the doctor as stress-free as possible for your cat (whether she's the shy type or not).

WHAT YOUR CAT IS TRYING TO TELL YOU

- *"This is a very scary place."* Most cats, especially indoor-only cats, have very limited exposure to new places. A veterinarian's office is not only foreign, but it's full of sights and smells that might frighten a cat.

- *"Are you trying to kill me?"* Your cat has no reason to trust the veterinarian, unless the two of them have developed a relationship. Previous trips to the vet's office were probably negative (very few cats have fun with the vet).

- *"I hurt!"* If your cat is injured or ill, he's not going to be his usual pleasant self. Unfortunately, vets often see animals at their worst. By helping your cat trust your vet, you can make those visits when he's feeling lousy seem less awful.

- *"Stay with me!"* Often vets will want to take the cat away from you to do procedures. You are the constant for your cat in this strange place, so being separated from you can be stressful.

HOW TO SAY IT

- *Choose your vet carefully.* Interview potential vets and ask how they deal with cats. Look for a patient and gentle vet. If your feelings toward the vet are positive, you'll have a better chance of engendering positive feelings in your cat. If you get a vet you like, try to see her consistently, which will lend stability to the experience for your cat.

- *Build rapport with your vet.* Be very involved with your cat's care and pleasant to work with. Don't hesitate to ask questions of your vet, but try not to be combative. A good relationship with your vet might allow him to give advice over the phone occasionally, which can help you avoid stressful trips to the office.

- *Seek out a feline-only practice.* If there's a veterinarian in your community who sees only cats, you'll avoid the waiting-room stress of dogs in the office. And your vet will be an expert in diseases that affect cats.

- *Give your cat the freedom to get comfortable.* If time allows, simply open your cat's carrier when you reach the exam room and allow her to leave the safety of the carrier at her own pace. When the exam is over, but while your vet's still talking with you, allow your cat to go back to the security of her carrier if she chooses.

- *Try a Tellington TTouch technique to get your cat out of the carrier.* After they arrive at the vet's office, many cats have to be dragged out of their carriers. To avoid that, take off the top half of a hard-sided carrier or zip open the top opening in a soft carrier (when that option's available) and put a towel on top of your cat. Start doing TTouch circles through the towel until your cat calms. Then wrap the towel around her, put her on the table, and keep doing touches. This is a much more gentle means of introducing your cat to the exam table.

- *Do some TTouch while you wait.* Calming TTouches will make your cat feel less stressed by the time the veterinarian gets in to examine you. If you're dealing with an emergency, and are using vigorous ear work to help your cat stay out of shock, stop at least ten minutes before the veterinarian examines your cat, since it can actually affect respiration and heart rate. You don't want to present a false picture to your vet.

- *Try some Feliway.* This product simulates facial pheromones that cats leave when they wipe their face against objects. Spraying some in your cat's carrier ten to twenty minutes before you put him in it can make the carrier seem like a safer place, since the familiar smell of pheromones will be within. With your veterinarian's permission, you can make the exam table less frightening by giving it a squirt of Feliway before letting your cat out of the carrier.

- *Use lots of treats.* Take along some really great treats to give your cat at the vet's office. She may be too stressed to take the treats, but if she can't, they might help her focus on something positive and distract her from the things that scare her.

- *Stay with your cat.* If he has to "go to the back" for procedures, ask your vet if you can go with him to help minimize his panic. Some vets will allow you to do this; it can be a comfort to your cat. Or perhaps your vet will just perform the procedure in the exam room, in your presence.

- *See if you can get a house call.* Some vets operate house-call practices, where they'll come to your home to treat your pets. This might be a way to get treatment for your cat without the stress of going to the vet's office.

- *Touch your cat at home.* Get your cat used to being touched, all over her body, especially her mouth and paws. You can do this with TTouch, with massage, or simply by petting.

HOW NOT TO SAY IT

- *Don't bring your cat in without a carrier.* Wrapping a cat in a towel isn't going to contain him well enough if he really wants to get away. It's also not going to make him feel safe around the other animals in the waiting room. Get a good, lightweight carrier that your cat can be comfortable in.

- *Don't avoid going to the vet because your cat doesn't like it.* If you think your cat is ill or has an injury that needs veterinary attention, bite the bullet and take her in. As with humans, early detection is very important in many diseases.

- *Don't take your cat out of the carrier until you're in the exam room.* You might feel your cat would be more comfortable if you opened the carrier's door in the waiting room. But a dog or another animal could try to give chase. Play it safe and keep your cat contained.

- *Don't give your cat any tranquilizers before going to the vet.* Even herbal calming preparations might affect your vet's ability to evaluate your cat. Rescue Remedy or other flower essences are okay, though.

- *Don't mask the evidence of illness.* If you're taking your cat to the vet for a specific problem, like an ear or eye infection, don't clean him up first. Your vet will want to see all the discharge and evidence of what's going on in your cat's body.

chapter twenty-five

Hairballs

Janice's cat, Elroy, leaves nasty surprises around the house: mushy, slimy hairballs. Much to her dismay, Janice sometimes steps in one in her bare feet when she gets up in the morning. As disgusting as that is, she's more worried about Elroy—are these nasty hairballs a sign that he is ill?

Cats ingest their own hair when they groom themselves. Their tongues are covered with tiny, backward-facing barbs, which catch the hair and draw it within. Nature designed cats' bodies to handle the hair and just pass it through in the stool. But thanks to humans, some cats have longer hair than nature intended. And others have tender stomachs. So instead of smoothly passing through the intestinal tract, the hair gets caught up in the gut and the cat throws it up. You can help your cat's system process the hair to make hairballs a thing of the past.

WHAT YOUR CAT IS TRYING TO TELL YOU

- *"I don't feel well."* What looks like a hairball might be something more serious. If your cat is throwing up hairballs more than once or twice a month, or sounding like she's vomiting hairballs but actually not producing any, see a veterinarian to make sure that the problem isn't something else.

- *"Please brush me."* Combing or brushing your cat regularly can remove excess fur before it can get inside your cat.

- *"I need more fiber."* Adding fiber to your cat's diet can help the hair pass through him.

- *"Chill out."* The occasional hairball, especially during shedding season, is nothing to worry about.

HOW TO SAY IT

- *Brush or comb your cat every day.* If you remove the shed hair for your cat, she won't be able to ingest it and form hairballs. If you're grooming daily and your cat is still vomiting up hairballs on a regular basis, try grooming twice a day. Or consider switching grooming tools (try a comb if you're using a brush, particularly if your cat has long hair). See the chapter on brushing and combing for information on making the grooming pleasurable for both of you.

- *Take your cat to the veterinarian.* If your cat is vomiting hairballs frequently, or if he sounds like he's trying to bring them up but nothing is coming out (which can be a sign of feline asthma), take him to the veterinarian to rule out any health problems. Hairballs that grow so large internally that your cat can't pass them through either end can cause serious constipation or even a blockage. If your cat is not eliminating regularly, take him to the vet.

- *Add some fiber.* Canned pumpkin (not pumpkin pie mix) is an easy way to increase the fiber in your cat's diet. It can help things (including hair) pass through your cat's intestinal tract more quickly.

- *Try a lubricant.* Hairball remedies, like Laxatone, are essentially flavored jellies that help lubricate your cat's system and help her pass the hair. Plain petroleum jelly can work, too. Just place some in a thin layer on your cat's shoulder, front leg, or other easy-to-reach area and your fastidious cat will lick it off. It can lubricate your cat as well. But don't use petroleum-based remedies more than once or twice a week, as they can interfere with the absorption of certain vitamins.

■ *Add some oils to your cat's diet.* The addition of essential fatty acids can help reduce shedding and thus cut down on hairballs. You can add oils like flax, fish, safflower, or evening primrose (available at health food stores). Or you can go to the pet-supply store and buy Mrs. Allen's Shed-Stop for cats, which adds essential fatty acids and reduces shedding.

HOW NOT TO SAY IT

■ *Don't give up on grooming.* If regular brushing of your cat doesn't alleviate the hairball problem, try using a different brush or a comb. Or increase the frequency. If your cat doesn't like to be brushed, try introducing it more gently and patiently. See the chapter on brushing and combing for more information.

■ *Avoid mineral oil as a hairball remedy.* While mineral oil may lubricate your cat's system and help him pass the hairball, it can be dangerous because a cat can aspirate it into the lungs.

■ *Don't rely on petroleum-jelly-based hairball remedies.* They can interfere with the absorption of fat-soluble vitamins (A, D, E, and K). Regular grooming should be your primary strategy in the battle against hairballs.

chapter twenty-six

Healthy Treats

Lee, like most pet owners, enjoys giving biscuits to her dog, Rex. She asks Rex to sit, then gives him a biscuit when he complies. All the while, her Manx cat, Gracie, watches. She's not sure, but Lee thinks that Gracie looks a little disappointed about not being included. But Lee is afraid to give Gracie treats because she doesn't know what kinds of treats are healthy for cats. Plus, Gracie doesn't sit when Lee asks her to.

It's just as much fun to give a treat to a cat as it is to give one to a dog. And certainly cats can be trained to sit (or do plenty of other things) for a treat. Don't let your cat miss out on the joy of being rewarded for her behavior. There are plenty of easy-to-obtain treats that are good for your cat and also great motivators.

WHAT YOUR CAT IS TRYING TO TELL YOU
- *"I like treats—even if I don't act like it."* If your cat turns down a treat, that doesn't mean she doesn't like any treats. With a little trial and error, you'll be able to find treats that your cat really enjoys—and is willing to work for.

- *"Show me the beef (or fish)."* The tiniest pieces of meat or fish (fresh or dried) can be a great treat for your cat.

- *"Don't mess with my nutrition."* Treats need to make up only a small portion of your cat's dietary intake. Even if the treats are made from healthy ingredients, they're probably not nutritionally balanced.

- *"Put it on the floor, please."* Unlike dogs, cats aren't adept at taking treats from your hand.

- *"I may be fat, but I still like treats."* You can provide treats even to your overweight cat, as long as they're lean and low-fat and you don't give too many.

- *"How about some variety?"* As in her regular diet, providing variety in treats is more healthy and helps keep your cat from becoming finicky.

- *"May I have a little of what you're eating?"* If you're eating something healthy, giving your cat a small tidbit can provide an instant training opportunity.

HOW TO SAY IT

- *Look beyond the cat-food aisle.* You don't need chemical-laden comercial cat treats to reward your cat. Healthy meat-based treats can be found all over the grocery store. Look in the meat department, the baby-food aisle, the ethnic food aisle, even the dairy case.

- *Learn to read a label.* If you want to give your cat commercial treats, know what's in them. Look for a simple label, devoid of chemical preservatives (like BHA, BHT, and ethoxyquin) and added sugars. You don't need to feed your cat candy!

- *Make your own treats.* It's easy to go to the grocery store, come home with a meat or liver, cut it into tiny pieces, and dry it in a low oven. Freeze what you can't use right away and you'll always have some cat treats at your disposal.

- *Look in Asian markets.* Explore the aisles of an Asian market for a variety of fish-related items that your cat would enjoy. Dried bonito fish flakes, for example, are used in making miso soup, so can be found where Japanese ingredients are sold. They make delicious treats and can also work as a flavor enhancer if your cat needs to be tempted to eat. They're also sold (usually at a higher price) in pet-supply stores and catalogs as Kitty Kaviar.

- *Think about dairy.* Unless dairy products give your cat diarrhea, you can use cheese (including cream cheese) as a treat. Cut or grate cheese into tiny pieces or give your cat a lick of cream cheese (or yogurt).

- *Use a spoon for the sticky stuff.* Cat treats don't have to be easy for you to pick up. Use a small spoon (your cat might prefer a rubber-coated baby spoon) to present meat baby food, cream cheese, or even canned cat food. Just give him a lick and put the spoon out of reach.

- *Try some anchovy paste.* You can find a tube of anchovy paste in the Italian section of your grocery store. Squeeze out a tiny bit and offer it to your cat to lick.

- *Buy some dried meats and fish.* Dried shrimp, minnows, even calamari are available as cat treats. You may be able to find them in an Asian market. If not, you can get them from *www.petextras.com*. Dried meats, like unseasoned jerkies, can be made at home or purchased from *www.pet extras.com* or from *www.sitstay.com*.

- *Harvest the power of catnip.* Many cats love catnip, and treats are available with it as one of the main ingredients. They're sold under the brand names Kookamunga and Cosmic, among others, and are available at pet-supply stores and websites.

HOW NOT TO SAY IT

- *Don't feed too many (or too large) treats.* Your cat only needs one tiny treat—not a mouthful—as a reward. If you give too many treats you risk messing with your cat's nutrition—and making him fat.

- *Don't discount the importance of treats in modifying problem behavior.* Treats are great for training, for rewarding desired behavior (like choosing to use the scratching post instead of the couch), for distracting a naughty cat from an undesired behavior, and for keeping a cat away from the door when you answer it.

■ *Don't expect your cat to take your treat from your hand.* Though you can certainly train your cat to do so, it might be easier just to drop a morsel on the ground in front of her, or offer a spoon laden with a sticky treat that your cat can lick.

■ *Don't reward your cat just for being cute.* Use the power of the treat to reward good behavior. See the chapter on clicker training for information on using treats to train your cat to do tricks and to solve behavior problems.

■ *Don't bother with junk food.* There are so many healthy treats available for your cat; don't fill him up with commercial treats loaded with sugar and preservatives.

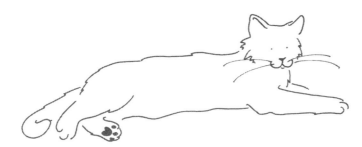

chapter twenty-seven

Obesity

Nicola's Maine Coon cat, Renoir, is a big boy. But with all that fur, Nicola didn't realize that Renoir was packing on the pounds until she took him in for his annual checkup and was shocked to see that he had gained four pounds over the past year! When she stepped back to look at him and feel the flesh under his thick coat, she realized she'd been fooling herself when she blamed his girth on his fur.

Many cats live sedentary lives. And many of them are overweight. A 1989 study of two thousand cats at thirty-one veterinary clinics in the Northeastern U.S., conducted by Cornell University, found that 25 percent of them were overweight. Being overweight is unhealthy for your cat. It can lead to diabetes, skin conditions, heart disease, even lameness. And being very overweight can shorten his life! According to a 1997 follow-up to the 1989 study, obese cats are twice as likely to die in middle age (between the ages of six and twelve years).

Since you control what your cat eats and, to a large extent, the exercise he gets, it's up to you to take care of his weight problem. Sometimes just a few dietary substitutions and more play time will do the trick.

- *"Feed me, feed me!"* Cats can be very adamant about being fed. And it often seems easier just to give in than to deny them an extra snack or two and listen to them complain.

- *"I'm hungry!"* If your cat's food isn't meeting his needs, he might be hungry all the time. If you fill his bowl whenever it's empty, he can put away a lot of food.

- *"I'm not well."* While weight loss is more often a sign of ill health in cats, weight gain without increased eating can also be a sign of a health problem.

HOW TO SAY IT

- *Do the rib test.* Not sure whether your cat's overweight? Feel his sides for his ribs. You should be able to feel them underneath his fur and skin. If you don't, there's a good chance he needs to lose some pounds. You can monitor his weight easily by weighing yourself while you hold him, then subtracting your weight.

- *Seek veterinary guidance.* Because too drastic a weight loss can lead to fatty liver disease, talk with your vet about a sensible weight loss program for your cat.

- *Play with your cat.* If you have a couch potato for a cat, it might just be because you haven't offered her anything better to do. As with humans, the key to feline weight loss is to increase exercise and decrease calories (a 1997 Cornell study showed that inactive cats are sixteen times more likely to be obese than active ones). Interactive play is a great way for your cat to burn some calories. It might take a little persuasion—your fat cat might not be anxious to move about—but search until you find a toy or game that strikes her fancy. And play with her every day.

- *Monitor your cat's food intake.* If he loses weight, make sure it's not because he's stopped eating altogether. Obese cats who stop eating develop a very real risk of fatty liver disease, or hepatic lipidosis, which happens when the body creates energy by moving fat from other parts of the body to make up for the energy not being supplied by food. This results in a buildup of fats in the liver and leads to liver dysfunction.

- *Stop the free feeding.* If your cat is overweight, she obviously doesn't know when to stop eating. Feed her a set amount on a set schedule. If feasible, smaller, more frequent meals will help her feel less hungry.

- *Feed wet food.* If you feed dry food, switch to a canned or fresh food. The higher water content in the food will help your cat feel fuller. Dry food is higher in carbohydrates, while canned food is higher in protein.

- *Feed high-quality food.* Commercial food with higher-quality ingredients is utilized better by your cat's system and you can feed less of it.

- *Measure your cat's food.* If you're trying to limit the amount you feed, don't eyeball it. Use a measuring cup or spoon (unless you're feeding a whole can at a time).

- *Use your cat's regular food for treats.* If you train your cat with treats (a great way to make him more interactive and help him lose weight), reserve some of his regular food to use for training treats. If you're feeding dry, store some in a canister with liver powder to make it extra special. If your cat's regular food is wet, you can let him lick a small amount off a spoon.

- *Treat differently.* Try some lower-calorie treats, like tiny bits of raw or steamed vegetables (if your cat considers them a treat), flakes of dried fish, or pieces of rice cake. Break your treats into the tiniest of pieces. After all, it's not the size of the treat, but the fact you're giving the treat, that pleases both you and your cat.

- *Have blood tests done.* If your cat is putting on weight, ask your vet to do a complete blood panel, to look for any metabolic problems that are making her unable to stabilize her weight by eating the proper amount. If no medical reason is found, your vet can provide advice on a weight loss program.

- *Don't cut down your cat's food dramatically.* Even if your fat cat looks like he could stand to miss a few meals, fasting him could actually lead to hepatic lipidosis (fatty liver disease). Talk to your veterinarian about the best feeding schedule while your cat is on a diet. And if he starts eating a lot less, watch for signs of jaundice and sporadic vomiting. If you see these signs, take him to the veterinarian immediately.

- *Don't switch to a "lite" food.* These dry foods tend to be higher in fiber and lower in fat and less nutritious for your cat, who requires meat and fat in her diet. Don't feed a diet food without consulting with your veterinarian first.

- *Don't free-feed.* If your cat is accustomed to eating whenever he wants—particularly if you have more than one pet—don't just leave the food down all day. Feed at designated times and remove any opportunity for your cat to steal the other animal's food by supervising all feedings.

- *Don't let your kids slip your cat food from the table.* That can certainly undermine your cat's weight loss program! Make sure that all family members understand the importance of your cat's diet.

chapter twenty-eight

Shedding

Donald and Kristen's apartment could have been featured in *Architectural Digest*. The dark furniture had sleek lines and the apartment was always spotless. But when they adopted Casper, their long-haired white cat, the illusion of perfection in their apartment was shattered. Clean as they tried to keep it, Casper's long white hairs were all over the furniture (and all over the couple's black clothing).

Cats shed. At least those with hair do. If you don't want any shed hair in your home, then you should either buy a hairless cat, get a reptile, or forget about pets altogether. If those aren't options for you, there are a few things you can do to keep shedding to a minimum.

WHAT YOUR CAT IS TRYING TO TELL YOU

- *"It's not my fault. I'm a cat. I shed."* Shedding is a perfectly natural process.

- *"Brush me!"* Regular brushing can help that hair come out on the brush, where you can remove it, rather than on your furniture or clothes.

- *"I could use some more fat in my diet."* Sometimes a dietary change can make a difference in shedding.

- *"I'm not well."* Excessive shedding can be a sign of a skin problem.

- *"I'm stressed out."* Cats can shed copious amounts under stressful conditions.

HOW TO SAY IT

- *Brush or comb your cat.* Daily brushing is the best way to keep shedding to a minimum. The hair comes out in the brush and you throw it away. If your cat has long hair, regular combing is especially important, since it prevents painful mats. Be sure to use the appropriate grooming tool for your cat's coat. (See the chapter on brushing and combing for more information.) Brushing also improves your cat's health, by stimulating the lymph system and aiding in circulation. It helps distribute the natural oils throughout your cat's coat. And it minimizes hairballs. Best of all, if you do it regularly, it becomes an enjoyable bonding time for both of you.

- *Take a trip to the pet-supply store.* A few products available through pet-supply stores and catalogs can help with the shedding. The Zoom Groom, a cat-shaped rubber currycomblike brush with long, flexible fingers, does a great job of getting shed hair off your cat. And cats seem to love the way it feels. Another product, the Purr Padd, is a white pad made of layers of soft polyester fibers that form an insulating cushion, which keeps your cat cozy and warm. Cats just love lying on it. The fibers of the pad are electrostatically charged, so they attract shed hair. If you put a few of these throughout your house, your cat might lie on them and leave hair on the pad instead of on your furniture. A product called Mrs. Allen's Shed-Stop provides essential fatty acids to reduce shedding.

- *Add some oils.* The addition of essential fatty acids to your cat's diet may make his coat glossier and help reduce shedding. You can add oils like flax, fish, safflower, or evening primrose (available at health food stores) to your cat's commercial or home-prepared food. You can feed him some canned salmon or mackerel on occasion to provide fish oil, or grind up flax seeds to provide ultrafresh flaxseed oil.

■ *Talk with your veterinarian.* Excessive shedding could be a sign of a skin disorder. If your cat's pattern of shedding increases noticeably—particularly if you see bald spots—a call or visit to the vet is in order.

■ *Make some dietary modifications.* An improvement in your cat's diet might help reduce the shedding. Improving protein content by providing higher-quality commercial food (one without additives) or feeding a home-prepared diet that includes human-grade meat can make the coat less brittle.

HOW NOT TO SAY IT

■ *Don't stress your cat out.* Frightened cats often shed more. So keeping things on an even keel might help reduce your shedding problem.

■ *Don't be irritated with your cat because of the cat hair all over your house.* That's not reasonable and it adds to your cat's stress.

chapter twenty-nine

Signs of Illness

When Mary's cat, Frisky, didn't live up to his name, she worried that he was a little under the weather. But he didn't seem dramatically ill— he was lethargic, he threw up a little, and he seemed to spend more time than usual drinking from his water bowl and using his litter box. But that was enough for Mary to take him in to see the veterinarian—and she was glad she did. The vet did some blood work and informed her that Frisky was suffering from kidney problems. He prescribed medication and an adjustment to the cat's diet.

Cats can be very quiet about their illnesses—they don't tend to draw attention to themselves when they feel ill. That's why it's so important for you to know the signs of illness. Like humans, cats benefit from early detection when it comes to disease.

WHAT YOUR CAT IS TRYING TO TELL YOU
- *"I may not look sick, but I don't feel good."* Signs of illness may be as subtle as unproductive visits to the litter box, increased appetite, or lethargy.

- *"I may hate going to the veterinarian, but take me anyway."* Most cats hate going to the vet. But if your cat is showing a sign of a problem, you need to overlook his antipathy.

- *"I need help now."* Familiarize yourself with the signs of an emergency so you know when to drop everything and rush to the vet.

HOW TO SAY IT

- *Watch your cat closely.* Keep an eye on her and take note of any changes in behavior, routine, or eating habits. If you see any of the following signs of illness, get her in for an exam:

  - Breathing through an open mouth (could be a sign of a heart problem)
  - Inability to use the litter box (for urine or feces) or pain or straining during elimination
  - Bleeding
  - Blood in vomit, stool, or urine
  - Keeping eye closed, eye discharge, or redness, or sudden blindness
  - Staggering or inability to walk
  - Persistent vomiting or diarrhea
  - Being unwilling to eat for twenty-four hours
  - Lethargy for twenty-four hours
  - Increased appetite
  - Lameness
  - Weight loss or gain
  - Increased water consumption and/or urination
  - Change in gum color (to white, blue, yellow, or bright red)
  - Seizures

- *Pay attention to your cat's litter-box habits.* Both excessive urination or, on the other extreme, the inability to urinate are signs of serious illness. Diarrhea and constipation should be noted, too.

- *Keep track of your cat's symptoms.* If you notice anything different about your cat, make a quick note in your calendar. This will help your veterinarian if your cat ends up needing medical help.

- *Be aware of the signs of an emergency.* These include stopped breathing, loss of consciousness, shock, gaping wound in the chest or abdomen, and severe bleeding. *The First Aid Companion for Dogs and Cats,* by Amy D. Shojai, is an excellent resource on dealing with emergencies. It also provides step-by-step care and first-aid instructions for 110 common injuries and conditions, from abdominal wounds to worms and everything in between.

- *Know where your closest after-hours veterinary clinic is.* If you need to take your cat to the emergency vet, you don't want to be searching the phone book to find it. Keep the address and phone number by the phone.

- *Use TTouch ear work during emergencies.* If you have to take your cat to the emergency clinic because he's suffered some sort of trauma, do fast, strong Ear Touches on your way to the clinic. Start with your hands on the base of each ear, with the thumb on the outside of the ear and the index finger on the inside. Using firm, strong strokes, move your hands up to the tips of the ear. Then take them off the ears and repeat. These touches will help improve your cat's vital signs and keep him out of shock. Stop doing the touches ten minutes before you see the veterinarian, to give the vital signs a chance to go back to where they were so that your vet gets a clear picture of the situation.

- *Monitor your cat's weight.* It's easy to pick your cat up and weigh the two of you on the bathroom scale (then subtract your weight) once a week or so. Since cats tend to be so small, a weight loss of only half a pound can be significant (that's 5 percent of the body weight of a ten-pound cat). Unexplained weight loss can be a sign of thyroid problem, so it's important to pay attention to your cat's weight.

- *Know how to take your cat's temperature.* A normal body temperature for a cat ranges from 101.5 to 102.5 degrees Fahrenheit. It's possible to take your cat's temperature rectally, if you're calm and gentle. Lubricate the tip with petroleum or K-Y jelly. With your cat on a table, lift his tail and gently insert the thermometer into his rectum. Calmly talk with him about what you are doing. Hold on to the thermometer and remove it after two minutes (unless you're using a digital thermometer, in which case you just wait for it to beep). Wipe it clean, read it, and use alcohol to clean the thermometer before storing it.

- *Use your cat's ear to take her temp.* Don't like the idea of taking your cat's temperature rectally? You can now get a thermometer that takes the temperature through the ear. This product, called Pet Temp, gives you an easy way to monitor your cat's (or dog's) temperature. See appendix for buying information.

- *Develop a good relationship with your veterinarian.* It's nice to be able to call your vet to find out whether you need to bring your cat in or whether it's something you can monitor at home.

- *Listen to your cat.* If she is giving you the feeling through her actions or her eyes that she doesn't feel good, pay attention.

- *Listen to your inner voice.* If your gut feeling is that something might be wrong, listen to it. While it's not good to stress your cat with an unnecessary vet visit, it's better than not taking him in for medical attention he needs.

- *Help your cat be comfortable at the veterinarian's office.* See the chapter on going to the vet for tips on making the vet visit more enjoyable.

HOW NOT TO SAY IT

- *Don't discount subtle signs.* Weight loss, lethargy, changes in urination habits, failing to use the litter box, failing to groom himself, excessive shedding, an increase in activity in an older cat, even a change in the smell of your cat's breath can be important indicators of ill health.

- *Don't panic.* You don't want to stress your cat by taking her to the veterinarian every time she sneezes. It's important to know the difference between an insignificant symptom (occasional vomiting) and something serious (vomiting more than once in a three-hour period). When you do take her, be as calm and positive as possible.

- *Don't be reluctant to go to the veterinarian because your cat doesn't like it.* If your cat needs medical help, he needs medical help. Instead, do your best to make the vet visit less stressful (see the chapter on going to the vet).

chapter thirty

Spaying and Neutering

Lisa and Sally live next door to each other with their respective cats, who are litter mates. Lisa loves her cat, Wallace, but he has habits that she finds very difficult to live with: he sprays the house, gets into fights when he goes outside, and defies her efforts to keep him indoors. Sally's cat, Joey, by comparison, has never sprayed—not even once. And he is content as an indoor-only cat. The main difference between the two cats? Sally had elected to have Joey neutered at a young age, while Sally kept Wallace intact.

Spaying your female dog or neutering your male is an essential component of responsible cat ownership. Unless you're participating in a well-planned breeding program with pedigreed cats, there's no reason not to spay and neuter. You don't want to be part of this country's staggering pet overpopulation problem (millions of cats are euthanized at shelters every year).

The benefits go beyond not contributing to the pet overpopulation problem. Neutered males spray less, wander less, fight less, and have a decreased risk of prostate cancer. Spayed females don't vocalize loudly like females in heat do, don't attract the attention of the neighborhood's tomcats, and will not develop uterine or ovarian cancer.

Spaying and neutering are common procedures. But they are surgical procedures that require anesthesia and therefore carry some risk. Knowing in advance what to expect after your cat has been spayed or neutered will help make the procedure less stressful for you and, by extension, for your cat.

WHAT YOUR CAT IS TRYING TO TELL YOU

■ *"Operate before I'm mature."* If you want to prevent spraying as well as mammary tumors in female cats, spay or neuter before your cat reaches sexual maturity. If you acquire an intact adult cat, however, don't hesitate to spay or neuter. It's never too late.

■ *"I'm uncomfortable."* Your cat will want to lick his or her incision after neutering or spaying. This is natural, but should be discouraged if the licking creates irritation or your cat starts pulling at the stitches.

■ *"Ouch!"* If your cat is in postsurgical pain, try a homeopathic remedy or talk with your vet about pain medication. Don't let your cat suffer.

HOW TO SAY IT

■ *Try some arnica.* Homeopathic *Arnica montana* is good for postsurgical pain. You can safely give the 30c potency (available at most health food stores) every couple of hours while your cat is in pain. Dissolve a few pellets in a tablespoon or two of water and either let your cat lap it up or put a dropperful into the side of her mouth.

■ *Keep an eye on the incision.* Examine it at least once a day for swelling, redness, or missing stitches. Call your vet if you see anything that worries you.

■ *Smell the incision.* Your nose can be a good detector. If you pick up that distinctive smell of infection, call your vet.

■ *Discourage excessive licking.* If your cat is licking like mad and disturbing the wound, gently distract him from doing so. Don't be harsh or punitive—after all, he's just trying to take care of himself.

■ *Try calendula ointment.* If your cat is licking a lot at her incision, gently dab some onto it. Available at health food stores, calendula is a natural

Why Should You Spay or Neuter Your Cat?

- To avoid being part of the pet overpopulation problem. Cats are very prolific. In just seven years, one cat and her offspring can bring forty-two thousand kittens into the world. Unless you're part of a responsible breeding program, there's no reason to bring more kittens into the world. Any that your cat bears will take homes from those who need them.

- Because breeding is not for the faint of heart. Breeding, done correctly, can be time-consuming, expensive, and sometimes difficult.

- It helps solve behavior problems like spraying, fighting, roaming, and excessive yowling and restlessness.

- It's healthy for the animal. Spaying and neutering eliminates the chance of uterine and testicular cancers and reduces the chance of mammary and prostate cancers. Plus, a neutered male is less likely to be injured fighting with other cats.

antibiotic. It won't harm your cat if she licks it and will help stop infection from setting in. It should also soothe itching.

- *Restrict your cat's activity level after spaying or neutering.* Put away the interactive toys for a few days and block off access to perches to help keep him from jumping too much.

- *Use Tellington TTouch.* If your cat is in pain, doing ear touches will be soothing and benefit her whole system. After she's no longer uncomfortable, do TTouch circles near the incision to speed healing.

- *Have your vet look at the stitches.* Even if they are supposed to be dissolvable, make sure your vet takes a look at the incision after a couple of weeks have passed. He or she can remove any stitches that haven't dissolved.

- *Try not to worry.* If you're stressed by your cat's surgery, your cat will pick up on it. Be upbeat when you leave her at the vet hospital.

- *Don't let your cat overdo it.* Follow your vet's advice about resting your cat after the surgery. He'll still be groggy when you bring him home, but he may be raring to go the next day. If your vet wants you to keep him quiet, discourage jumping and boisterous play. Try some relaxing massage or TTouch to keep him calm. (This goes for spayed females, too.)

- *If your cat is in pain (pacing, unable to get comfortable, crying out), don't let her suffer.* Either try homeopathic pain relief like arnica (detailed on the previous page), or call your vet about prescription or over-the-counter pain medication.

- *Don't use human pain relievers without your vet's approval.* Certain medications, like acetaminophin (Tylenol) and aspirin can be dangerous for cats.

- *Don't wait for a litter.* The notion that a female should have a litter before being spayed is a myth. There's no benefit to it, and, in fact, it's a detriment to her health. If you spay your female before her first heat, you'll greatly reduce the chances she'll develop breast cancer.

chapter thirty-one

Urinary Tract Problems

Hannah noticed that her cat, Wendell, was having difficulty in the litter box, straining when he urinated and sometimes crying out in pain. When she scooped the box, she realized he wasn't eliminating as much as usual. She waited until the weekend to get him to the veterinarian, and by the time they got there, poor Wendell wasn't able to urinate at all. The vet diagnosed a blockage, and Wendell had to have surgery to remove it.

Feline lower urinary tract disease (fLUTD) is an ailment that's all too familiar to many cat owners. (It was referred to as feline urinary syndrome (FUS) in years gone by.) It's actually not a single ailment, but rather an umbrella term for a variety of problems affecting the lower urinary tract. These include cystitis (bladder inflammation), struvite crystals and/or stones, and calcium oxalate crystals or stones. The crystals and stones can lead to obstructions. Because the male's ureter narrows as it reaches the penis, male cats are more prone to blockages. A stone can form a blockage, as can crystals when mixed with mucus to form a plug. This is life-threatening if not immediately treated. Educate yourself about LUTD so that your cat can get immediate treatment for this serious disorder.

131

- *"It's hard to pee."* Straining to urinate can be a sign of an obstruction. Don't confuse it with constipation.

- *"Ouch!"* Urinary tract problems can cause pain upon urination.

- *"The litter box is scary."* Cats might urinate outside the litter box when they have urinary tract infections because it hurts to pee and they associate the pain with the box.

- *"I'm stressed."* Stress can contribute to urinary tract problems.

HOW TO SAY IT

- *Be familiar with the symptoms.* fLUTD can be life-threatening for male cats who form a blockage as well as painful for cats who don't block. Know the symptoms and don't waste any time taking your cat to the vet when you see them. (See the "Feline Facts" at the end of this chapter for a list of symptoms.)

- *Know your stones: struvite (or "triple phosphate") crystals are the more common type; they form in alkaline urine.* Calcium oxalate crystals form in acid urine. Struvite stones can be dissolved with a special, temporary diet or medication, though surgery may be necessary. Calcium oxalate stones must be removed surgically. Some cats can actually have both types of stones simultaneously. Crystals may be present by themselves or in conjunction with stones.

- *Make sure your cat (healthy or otherwise) gets plenty of water or moisture from his food.* Keeping the urine relatively dilute is important for urinary tract health. Monitor your cat's water intake if you're feeding dry food. For cats who prefer to drink out of a running tap, look into the cat fountains, like the Petmate Fresh Flow or the Drinkwell, both available at pet-supply stores or through catalogs. These devices provide flowing, filtered water at all times.

- *Keep stress to an absolute minimum.* fLUTD is associated with stress, so keep your cat's life as peaceful as possible. Flower essences like Rescue

Remedy can be helpful in combating unavoidable stress. Anaflora flower essence company even makes a calming flower essence called Urinary Health, specifically to help with urinary problems. Green Hope Farm also has a flower essence for urinary tract health, called Flow Free. You can put a few drops of the flower essences in your cat's water or mix with water and mist over her.

- *Talk to a holistic veterinarian.* An alternative vet may be able to treat the urinary tract problems by finding any underlying problems that have manifested themselves in the urinary system and using modalities like acupuncture, homeopathy, and Chinese and Western herbs to balance the immune system and return your cat to health.

- *Try some nutritional supplements.* Antioxidants, cranberry extract, and glucosomine might be helpful in combating urinary tract problems. A holistic veterinarian can provide advice on which supplements to take.

- *Keep your cat's litter box squeaky-clean.* A dirty box might make your cat inclined to urinate less frequently, giving crystals and stones more chance to form.

- *Monitor your cat's litter-box habits religiously.* Scoop once a day, at minimum.

- *Use a special litter to check your cat's urinary health.* If your cat suffers from fLUTD, several special litters can help you monitor how he's doing. Scientific Cat Litter, a lightweight clumping litter, turns from pink to red if the urine Ph is abnormally alkaline, indicating a possible problem. Hemalert is a litter-box additive from Purina that changes color if there is blood in the cat's urinary tract. A special litter called Nosorb can help you if you need to bring a urine sample to your veterinarian. This litter is nonabsorbent, allowing the urine to pool so that you can collect it. All these products are sold through veterinarians.

- *Take your cat to the veterinarian at the first sign of a urinary problem.* Waiting can make the matter worse and treatment more difficult.

Feline Facts

Symptoms of Urinary Problems

If you see any of these symptoms of lower urinary tract disease, contact your vet immediately:

- Frequent visits to the litter box
- Urinating very small amounts
- Urinating outside the litter box
- Straining to urinate
- Pain with urination
- Inability to urinate

- Incontinence
- Blood in the urine
- Changes in urine color or odor
- Frequent licking of genitalia
- Ammonia odor to the breath
- Painful and/or distended abdomen
- Loss of weight or appetite

HOW NOT TO SAY IT

- *Don't feed dry food to a cat prone to fLUTD.* A 1999 study found that 39 percent of the cats who were fed a dry prescription food to combat urinary tract problems suffered a recurrence of the problems, as compared with 11 percent of the cats fed a wet form of the same prescription food. Dry food is by definition devoid of water. Cats who eat it produce urine that is more concentrated—making it easier for crystals to form.

- *Don't punish your cat for refusing to use the litter box.* Eliminating outside the box can be caused by a variety of issues, one of which is urinary tract infections. Rather than punishing your cat, get to the bottom of the problem. (See the chapter "Not using the litter box" for more information.) By yelling at your cat, you raise her stress levels, which can make the urinary problem worse.

- *Don't feed your healthy cats any of the special food you feed your fLUTD cat.* These specials diets are designed to acidify (or alkalinize) urine—you'll cause problems in your healthy cats if you allow them to eat this food.

chapter thirty-two

Vaccinations

Most responsible pet owners are familiar with the ritual of annual vaccinations. But more and more veterinarians (and pet owners) are starting to question the necessity—and even the safety—of annual revaccination. Clinical evidence doesn't exist to support the need for shots every year. And a connection has been made between vaccinations and an aggressive cancer known as vaccine-associated sarcoma in cats. At least one study suggests a relationship between vaccinations and immune-mediated kidney disease in cats. The American Association of Feline Practitioners and a number of veterinary schools recommend shots every three years in adult cats. Many holistic vets suggest minimal vaccinations, no more than a selected series of kitten shots, for example, except rabies when required by law.

The crux of the matter is that the duration of the immunity supplied by vaccinations is unknown. That's because precious few duration-of-immunity studies have been performed. But evidence suggests that shots last longer than a single year.

In 2002, the American Veterinary Medical Association released a report that said, "The practice of revaccinating animals annually is largely based on historic precedent supported by minimal scientific data. There is increasing evidence that some vaccines provide immunity beyond one year. Unnecessary stimulation of the immune system does not result in enhanced disease resistance and may expose animals to unnecessary risks."

In deciding whether to vaccinate your cat, do some research about the potential dangers of overvaccination, take into account the risk your cat has of contracting a specific disease, and talk to your vet about a schedule customized for your cat. The Vaccine-Associated Feline Sarcoma Task Force, sponsored by a consortium of veterinary groups, concluded that "Vaccination should be viewed as a medical procedure to be performed only after careful assessment of the needs of the patient, rather than as an automatic act dictated by the calendar."

WHAT YOUR CAT IS TRYING TO TELL YOU

- *"It may not look like it, but my body's reacting poorly."* An adverse reaction to a vaccination may not happen immediately after the shot and therefore might not be recorded, or even associated with the shot. But those shots, year after year, can have a cumulative effect.

- *"Don't give me a shot if I'm not feeling well."* Vaccines are labeled for use on healthy animals only.

- *"Do I really need another shot?"* Some experts contend that a single shot can afford a cat many years—even a lifetime—of protection. An indoor cat who is not exposed to cats outside his family is at very low risk. An older cat who has had many annual shots almost certainly doesn't need more.

HOW TO SAY IT

- *Talk to your vet about "titers," rather than another shot.* A titer is a blood test that measures the antibodies against a specific disease that are circulating in the bloodstream at the time of the test. If sufficient antibodies are measured, this suggests that your cat is protected. The trouble with titers is that they may tell you your cat is not protected even if he is. The antibodies need not be circulating in the blood in order to kick in when a cat is exposed to the disease. But an adequate titer can give you great peace of mind if you elect not to revaccinate.

- *Select vaccinations judiciously.* If you choose to vaccinate, you don't have to vaccinate against every disease for which a vaccine is available. Carefully assess your individual cat's risk and do some research about the efficacy and safety of the vaccines, particularly the newer ones. Vaccinate only against the diseases that pose a problem for your cat.

- *Separate the shots.* If you do choose to vaccinate your cat, don't overload her system with a combination shot. Instead, ask your vet to give a shot for a single disease (say, panleukopenia), then come back in two weeks for your next shot (like rabies). Give shots only for those diseases that are pertinent for your cat.

- *Get that annual exam.* Even if your cat doesn't need to get shots, he does need to see the veterinarian at least once a year. These wellness exams can help detect early signs of disease, give you an opportunity to ask questions, and help make your cat more comfortable with vet visits.

- *Do your research.* If you're going to question whether your cat needs to be revaccinated, go to your vet visit armed with information. The practice of annual revaccination is so ingrained into the veterinarian's practice that he or she might need to be presented with evidence that your questions are based on serious, not passing, concern. See the appendix for resources about the controversy surrounding annual revaccination.

HOW NOT TO SAY IT
- *Don't vaccinate if your cat is ill.* If you take your cat to the vet because she's feeling under the weather, resist any suggestion to get a booster to avoid another office visit. Shots aren't harmless—they provide a jolt to the immune system. If your cat's immune system is compromised by illness, that jolt could be harmful.

What Are the Signs of Vaccine-Associated Sarcoma?

According to the Vaccine-Associated Feline Sarcoma Task Force (VAFSTF), it is not uncommon for a small, firm, painless swelling to form under the skin at the vaccination site. It usually disappears after several weeks, leaving no effects. However, the lump can progress to a sarcoma (cancer). If you detect a lump, contact your veterinarian, who will want to send a small sample to a lab for biopsy if any of the following are true:

- The lump persists for more than three months after vaccination.

- It is larger than two centimeters in diameter (about the size of an olive)

- It is increasing in size one month after vaccination.

If the lump is found to be cancerous, your veterinarian may refer you to a veterinary cancer specialist.

You can learn more about vaccine-associated feline sarcoma and the VAF-STF, which was begun in 1996 as a joint effort of the American Association of Feline Practitioners, the American Animal Hospital Association, the American Veterinary Medical Association, and the Veterinary Cancer Society, at the VAF-STF's website, *www.avma.org/vafstf/default.asp.*

(*Source:* VAFSTF)

- *Don't vaccinate blindly.* By all means, take your cat to the vet when you get that postcard saying he's due for his annual exam. But don't automatically give the shots. Instead, talk with your vet about whether your cat really needs another vaccination. Do some research before you go to the vet, to familiarize yourself with the issue. By vaccinating judiciously, you could be saving your cat from serious illness (including cancer) down the road.

- *Don't vaccinate unnecessarily.* Many vets choose to give combination shots for the sake of simplicity. But does your cat really need every component of the shot? Talk with your vet about which diseases your cat might need protection against and don't give her shots for any others. If your cat is already protected from a disease by prior vaccination, another shot is not going to give her any added protection. And vaccinations aren't harmless: most contain adjuvants, such as aluminum hydroxide, designed to stimulate a longer immune response. Do you want to introduce these foreign substances unnecessarily?

■ *Don't combine vaccinations with other stressful procedures.* If your cat is at the vet for spay or neuter surgery (or any procedure requiring anesthesia), don't stress his body further by giving him a vaccination at the same time.

part three

Indoor-Outdoor Issues

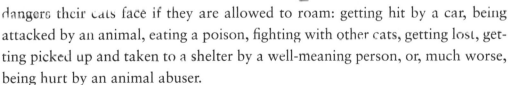

A big issue that faces many loving cat owners is whether they should allow their cats unsupervised access to the outdoors. Just as most responsible dog owners are committed to not letting their dogs roam outside, cat owners must take a hard look at the dangers their cats face if they are allowed to roam: getting hit by a car, being attacked by an animal, eating a poison, fighting with other cats, getting lost, getting picked up and taken to a shelter by a well-meaning person, or, much worse, being hurt by an animal abuser.

If you look at the statistics, it seems very cut-and-dried. Data indicate that indoor-only cats live a decade or more longer than indoor-outdoor cats. That's not surprising: common sense dictates that it's more dangerous for your cat outside.

It's not that easy, however, because many cats really want to spend time outdoors. But you can make the inside of your house more stimulating and interesting to your cat. And you can let your cat outside safely—if you invest some time and money in equipment to confine her outdoors, or train her to walk on leash.

If you find that your cat simply cannot remain content as an indoors-only cat—despite your best efforts—you may feel the need to let her out occasionally. If you do that, you must do it with the recognition that you may be shortening her life. And you must be certain that you can live with it if your cat does indeed die because of something she encountered outside. In some people's judgment, it comes down to a quantity- versus quality-of-life issue.

chapter thirty-three

Converting an Outdoor Cat into an Indoor Cat

When Sandy and Larry moved to a busy street in a new neighborhood, they realized that it wouldn't be safe for them to let their cat, Snickers, have free access to the outdoors as he did on their suburban cul-de-sac. But Snickers missed his access to the great outdoors and let them know it—loudly.

Turning a cat into an indoor cat is certainly possible. And it's often the right thing to do. (See the chapter on deciding whether to keep your cat indoors for an explanation of the benefits of keeping your cat inside.) But it can take a little effort, and a little patience, on your part.

WHAT YOUR CAT IS TRYING TO TELL YOU

- *"Hello? Did you forget how to open the door?"* If your cat was used to being let out upon request, he might ratchet up the volume in an effort to get your attention.

- *"It's boring in here."* It's up to you to try to make the indoors as interesting to your cat as the outdoors.

- *"Where am I supposed to go to the bathroom?"* If your cat always went outside to eliminate, you may need to acquaint him with the litter box.

HOW TO SAY IT

- *Make your home an indoor wonderland for your cat.* Make sure that you provide the following:

  - A scratching post (perhaps even one with bark on it, since he was used to scratching on trees)
  - A multilevel cat tree (since outside he was able to climb up to higher elevations)
  - Toys with which to amuse himself
  - Interactive toys you can play with together
  - A litter box with appropriate litter
  - Cat grass he can nibble on

- *Keep your cat occupied.* When you play with her using interactive, wand-type toys, you allow your cat to use her predatory instincts—something she was able to do on her own outdoors. Don't scrimp on play time. See the chapter on keeping your cat happy indoors for more ideas on indoor activities.

- *Clicker-train your cat.* It'll provide an outlet for his energy as well as providing mental stimulation, fun, and bonding for the two of you. See the chapter on clicker training for more information.

- *Talk to your cat.* Tell her why you feel the need to keep her inside and ask for her cooperation. Your intent, if not your words, will likely come through.

- *Try a flower essence.* Anaflora makes a flower essence called Essence of Nature, for indoor animals who are suffering from "nature deprivation." Put some in your cat's water, or mist it over him occasionally.

- *Do Tellington TTouch circles.* TTouch will not only help relieve stress that your cat might be feeling about not going outdoors, it will build the bond between the two of you.

- *Stick to your guns.* Turn a deaf ear to your cat's demands to go outside—use headphones or earplugs if necessary. If you give in after she's meowed for so long you can't stand it, you've taught her that all she has to do is keep meowing and she'll get what she's after.

- *Get a commitment from your whole family.* Every member of your family, including the children, needs to understand that the cat is not to be let outside. If necessary, post signs on the doors to remind them.

- *If possible, make the transition as the weather turns less temperate.* Your warm, cozy home should be more attractive to your cat when it's freezing cold outside.

- *Give your cat some safe outdoor exposure.* He can still safely enjoy the outdoors, in an enclosure or under supervision. See the chapter on options for safe outdoor experiences for suggestions on ways your cat can enjoy being outside safely.

- *Limit your cat's access to the whole house if she's not experienced with a litter box.* Provide soft, scoopable litter, which will probably be more similar to the soil she was used to using outdoors. Keep her in a room with her litter box (and food, water, scratching post, toys, and bed) until you're sure she's caught on to using a box. Be sure to interact with her in her room—you're not isolating her, just restricting her access to the house. Put a Feliway diffuser in the room to help her feel more comfortable.

- *Be careful going in and out the door.* If your cat is desperate to visit his haunts outside, he may make a run for it. See the chapter on bolting out the door for suggestions on ways to deal with this.

HOW NOT TO SAY IT

- *Don't punish your cat for protesting the situation.* She's just communicating her desires. If she annoys you in doing so, just ignore her. Don't yell at her for being upset that she can't go out. That will just upset her more.

- *Don't give in to your cat's protests.* If you let your cat out after a lot of caterwauling, you're encouraging the caterwauling. If he starts spraying, take measures to deal with it. (See the chapter on spraying.)

- *Don't ignore your cat's needs.* This might be a stressful time for her. Be sure to give her plenty of attention and outlets for her energy.

- *Don't neglect the litter box.* Be scrupulous in your attention to it. If he's used to eliminating outdoors where he can go anywhere, he won't want to use a dirty box. Scoop as often as you can, at least once a day.

chapter thirty-four

Deciding Whether to Keep Your Cat Indoors

Marvin, a solid black domestic shorthair, spends most of his time on the windowsill gazing at the activity outside. It breaks the heart of his owner, Michele, who worries that her cat would be much happier if he were allowed outside. Yet she signed an agreement with the rescue group from whom she adopted Marvin that she would never let him out. She knows that it's dangerous out there for cats, but can Marvin really be happy as an indoor-only cat?

When an adoption group insists that you keep your cat indoors, they do it for a reason. Statistically, cats who are kept indoors live much longer lives than cats who are allowed outside. But at what price? It depends upon the individual cat. Gazing out the window all day isn't necessarily a sign of unhappiness. It might be the sign of a cat happily entertained.

This chapter will help you weigh the pros and cons of indoor living for cats. The bottom line, however, is that keeping your cat indoors is something you should strive for.

- *"Keep me safe."* Indoor cats are exposed to fewer hazards than outdoor cats. It's as simple as that. If your cat is happy indoors, don't think twice about not letting him out.

- *"I'm bored in the house!"* Cats who yearn for the great outdoors might just lack stimulation inside. You can make the inside more interesting for your cat.

- *"I could use some company."* Sometimes getting a companion for your cat can help dampen her desire to be outdoors.

- *"Can't I go out sometimes?"* There are safe ways to let your cat experience some fun outside.

- *"I can't take it another second!"* Some cats are miserable kept indoors. For those cats, you have to weigh a very big issue: quantity versus quality of life.

HOW TO SAY IT

- *Take a hard look at the statistics.* In her book *Housecat: How to Keep Your Indoor Cat Sane and Sound*, author Christine Church sites statistics showing that the average life span of an outdoor cat is three to five years, while the average life span of an indoor cat is twelve to sixteen years. Keeping your cat inside will probably lengthen her life.

- *Know the risks.* By letting your cat outdoors, you're exposing him to a laundry list of potential hazards. They include:

  - Being hit by a car
  - Getting into a fight
  - Picking up an infectious disease, like feline leukemia (FeLV), feline immunodeficiency virus (FIV), upper respiratory diseases, or a host of other ailments
  - Being stolen
  - Getting lost
  - Being poisoned by antifreeze, herbicides, or other toxins

❑ Being attacked by an aggressive dog or human

❑ Being trapped in a basement or garage

■ *Start out by keeping your cat inside.* Hands down, it's the safest way for your cat to live. If your cat protests, try some of the suggestions in this book for entertaining him inside. Let him out under supervision. And know that if you relent and allow him free access to the outdoors, you're imperiling his health and safety.

■ *Provide environmental enrichment.* See the chapter on keeping your cat happy indoors for ideas on how to make life inside a lot more enjoyable for her.

■ *Keep him safe when he's outside.* Properly supervise your cat outdoors. See the chapter on safe options for outdoor experiences for ways you can let your cat out without endangering him.

■ *Talk to your cat.* If she's trying to slip out every time the door opens, sit down and tell her why you need her to stay inside. It might help her understand why it's important that she cease and desist her protests.

■ *Consult an animal communicator.* A professional communicator can help you feel that the message about the dangers of going outside has gotten through. And you can learn what your cat needs to be happier inside.

■ *Think about your pocketbook.* If you let your cat outside, he's bound to come home with injuries—or illness. It comes with the territory. You'll save a bundle on veterinary bills by keeping your cat inside, where he's safe.

■ *Get her a friend.* A feline (or even canine) companion might help your cat remain happier inside. Don't adopt a new pet without giving serious thought to the work and expense associated with welcoming another animal into your home Be sure to introduce the newcomer slowly.

■ *Follow your heart.* If you fully understand the dangers of letting your cat outside, yet you fear he can't be happy without free access to the outdoors, listen to your inner voice and make the decision that seems right for your cat. If you do let your cat outside, put a cat collar with an ID tag on him and have him microchipped (a permanent form of identification) so that if he's lost or picked up as a stray, you'll get him back.

HOW NOT TO SAY IT

- *Don't let an your cat outside if he or she is not neutered or spayed.* Cats are capable of procreating at a remarkable rate and this country's cat overpopulation problem means that millions of cats are euthanized every year. Do not contribute to this problem by letting an unaltered cat loose.

- *Don't let your cat outside if she is declawed.* To do so is to put her in even greater danger.

- *Don't let your cat go outdoors unsupervised without at least trying to keep him happy inside.* Some inside environmental enrichment and/or supervised access to the outdoors might be enough to keep him content (and safe) without needing free access to the out-of-doors.

chapter thirty-five

Keeping Your Cat Happy Indoors

S tacy lives on a busy street and knows that it's not safe for her gray tabby cat, Leonard, to go outside. Leonard doesn't try to sneak out the door, nor does he meow at the window. That's because Stacy knows the secret to Leonard's happiness: environmental enrichment inside the house.

Your house or apartment need not be boring for your cat. You can provide the mental and physical stimulation that he needs to stay happy. All it takes is a little bit of time and a little ingenuity and you can rest easy that your indoor cat is living his life to the fullest.

WHAT YOUR CAT IS TRYING TO TELL YOU

- *"I need exercise."* Cats certainly can get exercise inside, even in a small apartment. You just need to help.

- *"I need to hunt."* Your cat doesn't have to go outside to hunt—or at least to use her hunting skills. You can use toys and games to simulate hunting and satisfy that instinct.

- *"I need fresh air."* Do your best to see that your indoor cat gets to breathe fresh air during the pleasant times of the year.

- *"The outdoors is highly overrated."* Some cats have no desire to go outside. But that doesn't mean you shouldn't do your best to keep them stimulated inside.

HOW TO SAY IT

- *Play with your cat.* Cats are so much fun to play with—it's a wonder that so many people let their cats lead a sedentary life. Interactive toys (like wands with feathers attached to strings or fishing-pole-type toys), balls, or even a crumpled piece of paper with a string tied around it can provide endless enjoyment for both you and your cat. They're also an important way for your cat to satisfy his urge to hunt prey. Play with your cat at least twice a day. And be sure to put away any toys with strings so that your cat doesn't have unsupervised access to them. String can be very dangerous for a cat if swallowed.

- *Simulate hunting both mice and birds.* With your interactive toy, make the prey run along the floor and also fly through the air. Your cat is hardwired to hunt both, but may have a preference for one over the other. Keep things interesting by offering both types of prey (and a variety of toys).

- *Give your cat a tree to play in.* Cat trees, which are usually carpet-covered contraptions complete with perches, hideaways, and sometimes tunnels, are great fun for cats, who love to climb. Dangle a toy from part of the tree so your cat can bat it around. If your cat doesn't immediately take to the tree, don't give up. With a little time and subtle encouragement from you (put some catnip on it and try leaving treats for your cat to find when he decides to explore it), he should begin enjoying his new indoor jungle gym.

- *Give your cat window access.* If you don't have wide windowsills or furniture close to a window, you can buy a cat window perch at most pet-supply stores. The perches give your cat a comfortable place to lie and look out the window. Leave a blind up so that she can look out the window at night—there's plenty of fun stuff out there, like flying insects, for her to watch even at night.

- *Install a cat room that hangs out your window.* The Habikat is a plastic enclosure with windows on three sides that sits outside a window. It's about the size of a window air conditioner and installs in a double-hung window in much the same way. Your cat can sit in it and have a full, three-sided view of the outdoors. A vent provides fresh air. See the appendix for purchasing information.

- *Install a bird feeder near a window.* Watching birds can provide hours of entertainment for your cat.

- *Open the window occasionally—but be sure the screens are strong and tightly in place.* And do this only when you're home to keep an eye on things. An open window lets your cat enjoy the smells and sounds of the outdoors on a beautiful day.

- *Provide some hiding places.* Many cats love to hide. You can buy a den-like bed for your cat, a cat tunnel, or even just leave out a brown paper bag, tucked away behind some furniture.

- *Get a video.* If your cat pays attention to the television when it's on, you can play her a video with chirping birds and other intriguing subject matter to keep her entertained when you're not at home. One such tape, *Video Catnip*, is offered by *www.cattoys.com*.

- *Try a flower essence.* Anaflora offers Essence of Nature for the indoor animal who suffers from nature deprivation.

- *Think about a companion for your cat.* Another cat, or even a dog, might give him the company he needs to make the indoors sufficiently stimulating. Carefully consider this decision, however, since another pet requires a commitment of time and money for you. If you do get another pet, be sure to introduce him or her carefully. See the chapter on bringing home a new cat, and the one on cats and dogs if your new pet is a dog.

- *Let your cat outdoors—safely.* See the chapter on options for safe outdoor experiences for suggestions.

HOW NOT TO SAY IT

- *Don't make the door your greeting place.* Feline behaviorist Pam Johnson-Bennett in her book *Think Like a Cat* recommends establishing a special spot for ritual greetings. When you walk in the door, head for the spot, calling your cat behind you, and give her affection and a treat at that spot. Eventually, your cat will run to the spot when she hears your key in the door, minimizing her opportunities (or desire) for escape. See the chapter on bolting out the door for more strategies for preventing your cat from sneaking outside.

- *Don't leave your windows open when you're not home.* Cats can be killed falling out windows. Screens can give way to feline pressure, so be sure that any screens you have are sturdy. Keep your windows closed when you're not at home so that your cat doesn't escape.

- *Don't overdo the catnip.* This potent herb is a great way to get your cat interested in his toys or scratching post. But if you give him free access to it, its potency will wear off. Refresh your cat's toys perhaps once a week and keep the catnip in an airtight container, out of his reach, in the meantime.

- *Don't leave out the interactive toys.* Any toys with strings should be put away in a safe place and brought out only for your play sessions. String can be deadly if swallowed.

chapter thirty-six

Options for Safe Outdoor Experiences

Pinky, a once-feral cat adopted as a youngster, really wants to spend time outside. But her owner, Miranda, lives on a busy street and is unwilling to jeopardize her safety by letting her run free outdoors. Pinky cries at the window and Miranda has to be very careful every time she opens the door, for fear that Pinky will bolt through.

If you have a cat who's aching to go outside but can't be contained in your yard, there are options to allow her to go outside with you and stay safe while enjoying the sights, smells, and sounds of the great outdoors.

WHAT YOUR CAT IS TRYING TO TELL YOU

- *"Let me out!"* Many cats yearn to spend time outside and don't hesitate to let you know about it.

- *"Keep me safe."* You are the best judge of whether it is safe for your cat to spend time outside even under your supervision.

- *"I can cooperate."* You may think that asking your cat to walk on leash or stay in some kind of containment system outdoors is unrealistic. But cats can be taught to walk on leashes and can be safely contained by a variety of options now available.

HOW TO SAY IT

- *Leash-train your cat.* If you introduce the harness and leash slowly and with positive reinforcement, your cat can be taught to be comfortable on a leash. And that way the two of you can spend quality time outdoors together. (See the chapter "Walking on Leash" for tips.) If your cat is uncomfortable in a harness, he might better tolerate a Walking Jacket available from *www.hdw-inc.com.* These body-hugging nylon jackets provide more security and reassurance for cats than traditional harnesses.

- *Get a portable enclosure.* Kittywalks are mesh tunnels that allow a cat to walk around a bit without escaping (though they might not be escape-proof for the determined cat—be sure to supervise your cat in the enclosure at first). One version attaches to the grass with wickets, so your cat is walking on grass as she's enjoying being outdoors. Another version is available for patios and decks. The manufacturer also makes vertical enclosures with hammocks as well as accessories, like the covered cabana with a hammock inside that fits within the Kittywalk. (Available from *www.midnightpass.com.*)

- *Add to the fencing.* If you have a fenced yard, you can modify the fence by adding a barrier at or near the top that will prevent your cat from scaling the fence and climbing over. The Cat Fence-In system has a product that will prevent your cat from getting out and another that will also prevent stray cats from climbing over the fence into your yard (*www.cat fencein.com*). A similar product is available from *www.catfence.com.*

- *Make your trees unclimbable.* Cat Fence-In also markets tree guards that attach to the trunk of trees to prevent your cat from climbing it as a means of escape.

- *Make your own fence amendment.* The Kitty Klips Web site offers free instructions on how to use PVC pipe to cover fence supports and provide a slippery surface that cats can't sink their claws into, effectively thwarting attempts to scale the fence. Alley Cat Allies offers instructions for another do-it-yourself fence amendment at their Web site.

- *Create an outdoor play area.* You can purchase a "cat enclosure kit," essentially a six-by-six-by-six-foot redwood and galvanized wire enclosure with shelves for your cat to perch on, from C&D Products, LLC (*www.cdpets.com.*). Another company, CD&E Enterprises, makes large cages out of PVC tubing (or aluminum) and wire (*www.cde-animalcages.com*).

- *Take your cat for a walk in a stroller.* The makers of the Kittywalk outdoor enclosure also make a pet stroller that's essentially a tiny Kittywalk on wheels. It has a mesh part for fresh air and an enclosed part where a shy cat can feel secure.

HOW NOT TO SAY IT

- *Don't take any chances by leaving your cat outside unsupervised.* Cats are great escape artists; if your cat is an indoor cat, make sure his time outdoors is safe and supervised. This is doubly important if your cat is declawed.

- *Don't tie your cat out.* She could become entangled in a chain or cable. She could be vulnerable to other animals coming into the yard. She could wiggle out of her collar or harness and escape. She could become very frightened if left helpless in the face of potential predators. Your cat is much safer indoors than tied up outside.

- *Don't feel that your cat has to go outside if he's happy indoors.* Since it's safer inside, let your indoor cat stay indoors and provide enrichment for him through play, toys, and perhaps companions.

chapter thirty-seven

Walking on Leash

Susan's beautiful black cat, Boo, wants desperately to spend time outdoors. But she's committed to keeping him safe by not letting him roam free in her urban neighborhood. She tried putting a harness on him and taking him outside on leash, but Boo threw himself down on the ground and refused to walk. Susan figures that Boo just isn't a candidate for leash walking. She may be wrong.

Most cats aren't the natural leash walkers that dogs are. But if you introduce the harness and leash gradually and are patient, you and your cat might be enjoying walks together. If your indoor cat is longing to spend more time outdoors, it can be worth the effort: leashes not only provide your indoor cat safe opportunities for being outside, they're an important safety net if you travel with your cat.

WHAT YOUR CAT IS TRYING TO TELL YOU

- *"Get this thing off me."* The harness and leash might feel restrictive to your cat.

- *"What's going on?"* The harness might feel so foreign to your cat—particularly if you put it on him without introducing it first—that he refuses to move with it on.

- *"Thanks for taking me outside."* If your cat is yearning to be outside, she should appreciate the excursions once you've accustomed her to a harness and leash.

- *"I'm not a dog."* Even if your cat becomes accustomed to leash walking, he's not going to want to walk by your side and go where you want. Instead, he'll walk you.

HOW TO SAY IT

- *Introduce the harness and leash slowly.* Let your cat get familiar with these objects before you put them on her. Let her sniff and just coexist around the harness. If you clicker train her, click if she touches the harness. Once she's comfortable around the harness, try gently putting it on her. Click and treat for calm behavior with the harness on. Let her wear it in the house for short periods of time, to get her used to it. Be sure to reward her for tolerating it.

- *Start young.* Generally, the younger your cat is when you start leash training, the easier it will be. This might mean having to purchase more than one harness as your cat grows. If you start while your cat is still a kitten, make sure he hasn't grown out of his harness—you want it to be snug, but not uncomfortably so.

- *Select a sturdy, comfortable harness.* Avoid harnesses with elastic, which can be binding. Buy a harness that attaches at the top so that you don't have to fumble around your cat's belly to buckle or snap it. An H-shaped harness is more secure and comfortable for most cats. To select the right size, measure your cat's girth, at the largest part of his rib cage.

- *Look at harness alternatives.* The Walking Jacket from HDW Enterprises is a nylon harness that is more like a jacket. It's harder (though not impossible) to get out of than harnesses. And for some cats, it adds an extra feeling of security. Other cats might find it more annoying than a harness.

- *Test the harness before you buy it.* Pull at the harness (hard!) to test its strength. See how easy it is to adjust and make sure any adjustable buckles don't adjust on their own. Test how easy it is to fasten and release the connectors.

- *Select a leash made for cats, not dogs.* Even leashes made for small dogs probably have a larger clasp than your cat will find comfortable. At least at first, restrict yourself to a six-foot leash, which will give you more control over where your cat goes.

- *Try a T-shirt on your cat first.* You can get your cat accustomed to wearing something while at the same time calming her by putting a T-shirt on her. T-shirts help animals feel more secure, according to Tellington TTouch practitioners. Use an appropriate-size baby's T-shirt (don't forget about preemie sizes), put on backward.

- *Take your first "walk" inside the house.* For safety's sake, don't take your cat outside on leash right away. Walking her in the house will allow you to safely see whether she's going to find a way to wriggle out of the harness and whether the harness fits properly.

- *Carry your cat in and out the doors.* Don't give him the idea that it's ever okay to walk out an open door on his own.

- *Stay close to home on your walks.* If you stay in your own yard (or very close to it), there's less chance your cat will get spooked by other animals, kids on skateboards, or other potentially scary things. You don't want her pulling the leash out of your hand and running away.

- *Think about leash training even if you're not planning to go on regular walks.* The leash can be a backup safety device when you travel with your cat. If your cat is comfortable with a leash and harness, you can leash him up inside hotel rooms, for example, when you have to open the door to let someone in.

- *Watch your cat's body language.* Is she comfortable outside on the leash? Is she experiencing sensory overload? Let your cat wander at her own pace. If she seems unhappy at all, bring her inside. Keep things upbeat and offer her treats while she's in the harness, to help make her more comfortable.

- *Keep an eye out for danger.* Be hypervigilant about possible safety hazards or things that might frighten your cat while outside. Dogs (even those on leash) might send your cat into a panic. Same goes for small children and loud noises. Particularly if your cat is a novice at being outdoors, you want to try to protect him from frightening experiences. Calmly scoop him up and take him away if he perceives that he's in danger.

HOW NOT TO SAY IT

- *Don't attach the leash to a collar.* Collars aren't safe for leash-walking cats, who are adept at wriggling out of them. Always attach the leash to a harness designed for cats. Do use a collar, however—and attach an identification tag to it. That's an important safety precaution in the event that (despite your best efforts) your cat gets out of her harness.

- *Don't wait until the day you need to use the harness to introduce it to your cat.* Expect that it will take a few days to get him comfortable around, then in, the harness before you attach the leash and take him outside.

- *Don't pull on your cat's leash, especially at the beginning.* Walk with her where she wants to go. If you need to direct her, use a food lure rather than dragging her. You want to keep these walks fun!

- *Don't wait for your cat to go to the bathroom on your walks.* Fastidious cats wouldn't be inclined to eliminate with you at the other end of a six-foot leash. Let your cat do his business in the litter box as usual.

- *Don't expect your cat to walk like a dog.* Unless you put a whole lot of time into training that behavior, she's not going to walk by your side. She'll walk out in front of you, sniffing and exploring. Just accept your role as a cat follower and don't expect to get any exercise on your walk. Your job is to keep your cat safe.

part four

Solving Specific Behavior Challenges

No cat behaves perfectly all the time. Many cats are behaving according to their natural instincts when they "misbehave." If you have a problem or two with your cat, you may have tried yelling or punishing. You've probably noticed it doesn't have a lasting effect. Many problems can be addressed by either management (taking away the opportunity for your cat to do the undesired behavior) or redirecting your cat to an alternative behavior. By reinforcing the behavior that you want and making it difficult for him to do things you don't like, you maximize the chance that the problem behavior will disappear.

Many problems with cats are related to stress. Cats are exquisitely sensitive creatures and seemingly minor changes can cause them to do things we don't like, like scratching the furniture, spraying, or not using the litter box. Minimizing stress and helping your cat stay calm through the use of simulated feline facial pheromones, interactive play, hands-on therapies, and simply keeping life on an even keel can help keep problem behaviors from starting in the first place.

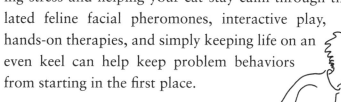

chapter thirty-eight

Biting and Scratching People

Lisa loves her cat, Angel, but sometimes she thinks he's actually a devil! She'll walk down the hall and the young Abyssinian will leap out and grab her ankles—with his claws out. Or she'll be petting him and suddenly, out of nowhere, he'll attack her hand with his claws and teeth.

Cats will bite and scratch for a variety of reasons. Sometimes it's because they're scared or in pain. Other times it's because they're overstimulated. They might attack because they see something they can't attack (like a cat outside the window), so they go after the nearest thing they can get to (even if it's you). Maybe they're just playing. Or you might have an aggressive cat on your hands. The way you should deal with biting and scratching depends upon why the cat is doing it.

WHAT YOUR CAT IS TRYING TO TELL YOU

- *"I hurt."* A cat who is in pain doesn't want to be touched and will use his teeth or claws to keep you from touching him.

- *"I'm scared."* A fearful cat will attack if she feels that's her only option to defend herself.

- *"I've had enough petting, thank you."* If you're petting a cat and he suddenly starts biting and clawing, he's overstimulated. He probably already gave you some subtle signals that he'd had enough.

- *"If I can't attack my real enemy, I'll attack you!"* Redirected aggression happens when a cat turns on a human or other cat when she's stimulated by something she can't get to.

- *"Kittens just want to have fun!"* Some cats—particularly young cats—will pretend you're their prey and attack you for the sheer fun of it.

- *"Pay attention to me!"* Sometimes a cat will take a little bite when you're not giving him the attention he craves.

- *"I'm mean."* Some cats, like some dogs, are aggressive. You might need professional help to rehabilitate an aggressive cat.

HOW TO SAY IT

For the cat who is in pain:

- *If your cat is lying in a defensive posture, low to the ground and claws at the ready, with his flat ears back against his head, he needs help.* You need to get him to the veterinarian—but first he needs to calm down. Leave him alone and put his carrier on the floor in the room with him, with the door or flap open (you might try squirting Feliway in each corner, which will calm him when he enters it). Your cat might view the carrier as a safe haven and enter it. If he does, close the door and get him to the veterinarian, who can examine him to find the source of the pain. If he doesn't, let him calm down and see if you can approach him and put him in his carrier as you usually do. If you're afraid you can't do that without getting hurt, call your veterinarian for assistance.

- *Try some Rescue Remedy.* Put a few drops of the Bach Flower Rescue Remedy in a spray bottle or plant mister and gently spray the air around your cat to calm him. Don't spray a stream of water right at your cat—that will only frighten him.

For the fearful cat:

- *If your cat is afraid, her posture will be similar to the pained cat, on the previous page.* The hair on her back might go up and her tail might even puff out. Her pupils will be dilated, and her whiskers flattened back. She might be hissing or growling. She'll put her body sideways from you, but turn her head to face you. If this describes your cat, leave her alone. Comforting her might prompt her to hurt you—she's not in her right mind. Just leave the room and let her calm down. Don't start interacting with her again until she's behaving normally.

- *Put some Rescue Remedy in her water.* A few drops in her water bowl might help calm her tendency to get scared. If she drinks it throughout the day, she may feel more secure.

- *Face the fear.* If you know what is triggering the fear in your cat, talk with a veterinary behaviorist about putting together a program of desensitization and counterconditioning to make your cat more comfortable.

For the overstimulated cat:

- *If your cat sinks his claws or teeth into your hand while you're petting him, freeze.* By jerking your hand away, you might get injured. Instead, try to distract him with a toy or happy talk. After your cat withdraws his claws and/or teeth, move your hand away, put him down, and walk away. Your cat has effectively ended the petting session.

- *Learn to read your cat's warning signs.* It may seem that out of nowhere, he is turning a beautiful moment ugly. But he probably gave you plenty of notice that he was ready for the petting session to end. Watch his tail. If it starts swishing back and forth or thumping, stop petting him. Another sign is shifting of body position. And skin twitching. If you see any of these warning signs, stop petting him, though neither of you needs to relocate. Try to know your cat's limits so you can end the petting session before your cat has to warn you to stop.

- *Know where your cat likes to be petted.* If he bites you (or warns you) when you stroke his tail, then don't stroke his tail.

- *Do Tellington TTouch instead of petting.* Rather than just petting your cat when he sits in your lap, do some TTouch circles in random places on his body. This is not only a loving touch, but a healthful one, too, aiding your cat's cell function and helping his nervous system to work more smoothly.

- *Recognize each cat's individuality.* Every cat will have a different threshold. Just because Cat A enjoys being petted for five minutes doesn't mean that Cat B will tolerate it for that long.

- *Be careful with belly rubs.* If your cat offers his tummy for a belly rub, you can oblige. But he might quickly have enough. Watch for signs that he's through and withdraw before he grabs you.

For redirected aggression:
- *If your cat goes after you because she's all worked up over seeing another cat in her yard, you're dealing with redirected aggression.* (If one of your other cats had approached the stimulated one, he would have been the victim.) Leave her alone until she's calmed down which may take several hours. Better yet, don't approach her when she's stimulated this way.

- *Block access to the window, at least for the short term.* Close the blinds or even cover the window with cardboard, if necessary. This will allow your cat to calm down without being charged up again by the intruder.

- *Talk to your neighbors about keeping their cats inside.* Explain to them that indoor cats tend to live longer lives. If the neighbor cats are kept indoors, redirected aggression should become less of a problem.

For the play attacker:
- *If your cat attacks your ankles—pouncing out at you when you're not looking, then tearing away—he's just trying to play.* To keep your ankles safe, spend more time playing with your cat. Using interactive toys, play with your cat several times a day.

- *If you can see your cat coming and anticipate an ambush, toss a toy ahead of you to divert her.*

- *Consider adopting a feline companion for your cat to play with.* If he is home alone all day, he might be play-deprived (and thus focused on your ankles). Be sure to give careful consideration before adding a pet, however, since you'll be making a commitment of a dozen years or more.

For the attention seeker:
- *The cat who takes a bite at you while you're sitting at your computer or watching TV is trying to get your attention.* Too bad he's chosen a painful way to do it! When this happens, remove all your attention from him. Turn your back on him, or walk away, if necessary. By giving him any attention at all—even by yelling at him—you're rewarding him for the misbehavior. After a short while, give him the attention he craves—on your terms rather than at his (pain-inducing) command.

Unprovoked aggression:
- *If your cat behaves aggressively toward you for no discernible reason, have him checked out by a veterinarian to rule out a medical cause.* If a medical reason can't be found, ask your veterinarian for a referral to a behaviorist who can come to your house to try to find a reason for the biting or scratching. If necessary, get a recommendation from a veterinary university in your state.

- *Talk with your veterinarian or veterinary behaviorist about drug therapy for your aggressive cat.* Or talk with a holistic vet about herbal therapies. Sometimes this kind of intervention can calm an aggressive cat and can help make a program of behavior modification more workable.

HOW NOT TO SAY IT
- *Don't interact with a cat who is acting aggressively.* No matter what the reason for the biting or scratching, interaction with you will only make it worse.

- *Don't get mad.* Rather than taking it personally, examine why she is lashing out and try to address the problem.

- *Don't punish your cat for aggressive behavior.* Violence begets violence. Physical punishment will only frighten your cat, contributing to more aggression. (For that matter, never physically punish any cat, no matter how he's behaving.) Even a tap on the nose can be perceived by your cat as aggression on your part.

- *Don't let your cat bite your fingers in play.* She shouldn't view your fingers—or any of your body parts—as toys. If she bites your hands in play, gently remove your hand (moving it toward, not away from, your cat's mouth and claws to extricate it) and either end the play session or give her an appropriate toy—like a plump catnip mouse—to bite.

- *Don't live in fear of your cat.* If your cat's behavior is frightening you and having a negative effect on your relationship, hire a behaviorist to come help you pinpoint and solve the problem.

chapter thirty-nine

Bolting Out the Door

Mitsy, an indoor cat, streaks out the door whenever it is opened. Before the person opening the door knows what's happened, the gray cat is out and not in a hurry to come back. Her owner, Lou, is committed to keeping Mitsy safe by keeping her indoors, but faces a challenge every time he comes in the door—or opens it for a guest.

Bolting out an open door is a dangerous habit for a cat. It can be difficult to train a determined cat to stay away from the door, but you can take some measures to help with the problem.

WHAT YOUR CAT IS TRYING TO TELL YOU

- *"The outdoors beckons!"* It's fun to get out and explore the neighborhood. Cats who really want to go out will jump at every opportunity.

- *"Why shouldn't I?"* If you give your cat the opportunity to bolt—and he's a confirmed bolter—what's to stop him?

- *"Make it worth my while to stay inside."* Your cat might be willing to stay away from the door when it opens, if you reward him for it.

- *When you enter your home, reward your cat at a safe distance from the door.* Feline behaviorist Pam Johnson-Bennett, author of *Think Like a Cat,* suggests that you set up an interior location where you always greet your cat. A cat tree is an excellent spot. When you walk in the door, stride right to that greeting place, then greet your cat and give him a treat. Soon he'll trot to that spot when he hears your key in the door.

- *Keep delicious treats near the door.* Or in your pocket. That way, as you approach the door with your cat, you can toss a treat away from the door, giving you time to open it for your guest while your cat is occupied with the treat. It could turn into such a fun game that the doorbell becomes her cue to wait for the treat toss. When you come home, try tossing a treat as you enter the door so that your cat doesn't streak out between your legs. Even better, teach your cat to go to her spot when you come home, then give her the treat there.

- *Toss a treat or toy for your cat to get him away from the door so you can leave.* Or leave him a treat or two in his cat tree, to keep him occupied while you make an exit.

- *Limit access to the door.* If you have a confirmed bolter, close your cat into a room away from the door when the doorbell rings. This might take a little effort, but the effort will be worth it if it keeps your cat out of danger.

- *Give your cat safe exposure to the outdoors.* Satisfy your cat's need to go outside by taking her out on leash or installing a cat walk in your yard. See the chapter on options for safe outdoor experiences for other ideas. Your cat is telling you that she craves some outdoor time.

- *Train your cat to come when called in the event he gets out.* Cats can be trained—and certainly most cats already come when you start opening a can or bag of food. Put it on cue and you might have a better chance of retrieving your cat should he sneak out on you. See the chapter on clicker training for more information.

- *Consider an indoor collar (or harness) and leash.* If you don't have a physical way of keeping your cat away from the door (like eliminating his access) you can keep a leash attached to a puppy collar hanging from the doorknob and put it on your cat before you open the door. You might want to put a sign on your door suggesting guests be patient, since it might take you a little while to get your cat leashed up.

HOW NOT TO SAY IT

- *Don't greet your cat at the door.* Instead, go right to your predesignated greeting spot (like a cat tree), ignoring your cat until you get there. Once you're both there, greet him enthusiastically and give him a treat.

- *Don't punish your cat when she does come back.* If your cat gets out, welcome her back with open arms. There's no better way to discourage your cat from coming to you than punishing her (physically or verbally) when she does.

- *Don't damage your relationship by using aversive means to keep him from the door.* It might work to spray your cat with a squirt gun when you enter the door or to scare him away from the door by throwing something at him. These tactics—particularly when they're used as you enter the door—could have a lasting negative effect on the way your cat feels about you.

chapter forty

Clawing the Furniture

David loves his cat—but he also loves his brand-new couch. Unfortunately, his cat, Mindy, loves it, too! Mindy's taken to sharpening her claws on the side of the couch and nothing David has done has effectively dissuaded her.

Scratching is as natural as breathing to a cat. Cats have a genuine need to scratch, and they'll pick the surface that's most appealing to them. All you have to do to save your furniture is to provide an appropriate surface that your cat will prefer.

WHAT YOUR CAT IS TRYING TO TELL YOU

- *"I'm keeping my claws in shape."* Scratching allows your cat to remove the outer dead nail sheath. Cats' claws are their first (and most important) line of defense and it's natural for them to keep their claws in shape.

- *"I'm stretching."* Clawing both exercises and relaxes your cat's muscles in her feet, forelegs, and shoulders.

- *"This feels good."* Scratching can be an emotional release for your cat as well. Think how good a long hard stretch feels to you.

- *"This is my territory."* Some cats claw in order to mark. Cats have scent glands on their paws and scratching leaves a little of their scent behind for other cats to smell. Scratching also leaves a visible mark on the object scratched.

HOW TO SAY IT

- *Provide a scratching post your cat will like.* Make sure it's sturdy (if it falls over while your cat is scratching it, it'll never be used again). Make sure it's made of rough material (no matter how ugly that material may be) that your cat can really sink his claws into, like the back of a rug or tightly wound rope. Remember that a cat's wild relative, the tiger, enjoys clawing trees! And make sure it's the proper height. If it's too short and your cat can't stretch to full length, it might frustrate him; at the very least your cat won't be getting optimal benefit from using it.

- *Provide more than one scratching place.* Good, solid, tall scratching posts can be expensive. But you can supplement the primary post with smaller cardboard or sisal pads available at pet supply stores. Putting one next to a favorite scratching chair might take care of the problem—and give you a handy place to redirect your cat if you should notice him considering clawing the furniture.

- *Put the scratching post where your cat will use it.* When does your cat like a good scratch? After he gets up from a nap? Then put the scratching post near where he sleeps. After he eats? Put one by his eating place. If he has a favorite piece of furniture he likes to scratch, place the new scratching post near it.

- *Encourage your cat to use the post.* If she doesn't approach the new post, try scratching it yourself to attract her attention. When she does scratch the post, quietly praise her as she scratches.

- *Try catnip.* Some posts come with catnip embedded in them. If yours does not, try sprinkling some irresistible catnip to attract your cat to the post. Refresh it weekly.

- *Play with your cat.* Entice him to touch the scratching post by playing with him near it. Use a cat toy such as a feather or toy on a string dangled on the post so that when his feet inevitably touch the post he gets to feel how great its texture is. (Be sure to put away the toy when you're not using it together so that the string doesn't injure your cat.)

- *Reward your cat for using the post.* Praise him and give him a treat when you see him scratching in sanctioned areas. That should encourage him to keep up the good habit.

- *Spray some Feliway where you don't want your cat to scratch.* Spritz your cat's favorite inappropriate scratching haunts with Feliway, a simulated feline facial pheromone, to discourage repeat scratching. Cats don't tend to scratch places they've marked with their faces. You can also spray it preventively on furniture that your cat might find attractive. The manufacturer says the spray will not stain or mark furniture, but recommends testing in an inconspicuous area, just in case.

- *Trim your cat's nails.* This way, if she does claw the furniture (or you), the damage won't be so great. See the nail-trimming section of this book.

- *Discourage his old haunts.* If providing a sanctioned place to scratch and encouraging him to use it doesn't work, apply double-sided tape, a product called Sticky Paws (which is basically wide strips of double-sided tape), or tape some foil over clawed areas of your furniture. This makes these surfaces less attractive for clawing. If the scratching persists, put something under one leg of the furniture to make it unstable and therefore less appealing to scratch. But don't do any of this unless you supply a sanctioned place for your cat to scratch. He needs to scratch, and if you don't give him a place to do it, he'll just find his own.

Declawing

Is declawing the answer to shredded furniture? It's a controversial question. But most everyone can agree that declawing—if done at all—should be done as a last resort.

Declawing a cat is not a simple matter of quickly removing the claws. Cats' claws are retractable and are therefore complicated mechanisms. The declawing procedure actually removes bone as well as claws. It's akin to having your fingertips amputated below the first knuckle.

Cats who are declawed lose their main source of defense. Many are stressed by not being able to defend themselves and not being able to use their paws properly. Some vets refuse to declaw. Others will perform the procedure when the only alternative is rehoming the cat or euthanasia. It's illegal in a number of countries.

Providing your cat with something to scratch besides the furniture—and persevering until you find the right scratching post—is a simple alternative to what many describe as a gruesome and inhumane procedure. If you're considering declawing your cat, consult a feline behaviorist first.

See the chapter on declawing for more information on the procedure.

HOW NOT TO SAY IT

- *Don't try to force your cat to scratch the new scratching post by picking up his paws and placing them on the post.* Cats hate that, and it will just create negative associations with the scratching post.

- *Don't holler at your cat when you catch him scratching the furniture.* That will only damage your relationship by making him not want to be in the same room with you. Instead, calmly take him to his scratching post and make a note of when and where he scratched the furniture, to help you figure out where to put the post.

- *Don't make a scratching post out of leftover carpet from your house.* No need to confuse your cat about which of the identical carpets is okay to claw. Besides, carpet tends to be too soft to make a great scratching post (though some cats do like it).

- *Don't give up.* If your cat isn't using the scratching post, that just means you haven't found one that's more attractive than your furniture. Where on the furniture is he scratching? If it's on the cushions or the back, he may prefer a horizontal scratching post that lies on the floor rather than standing on end. If one scratching post doesn't do the trick, try another. Your cat might prefer a different material.

- *Don't be stingy.* You might need more than one scratching post, particularly if you have more than one cat. If your cat's using the scratching post only sporadically (and scratching places you find less desirable the rest of the time), you may want to buy (or make) more.

chapter forty-one

Excessive Grooming

Janet's Russian Blue, Dusty, grooms himself to the point of leaving bald patches and sore spots. Janet tries to discourage his grooming, but the cat is intent on it and spends much of his waking time licking and chewing on himself.

Most cats spend a lot of time grooming themselves. Their fastidiously clean nature is one of the things that make them such great indoor companions. But if your cat is actually making himself bald with his grooming, he may have a physical problem. Or he may be stressed out. A visit to the vet is in order. If he gets a clean bill of health, there are things you can do to help alleviate his stress.

WHAT YOUR CAT IS TRYING TO TELL YOU

- *"I'm not well."* An underlying medical condition can cause excessive grooming. The first thing to do is to have your cat thoroughly checked out by a veterinarian.

- *"I'm stressed."* If your cat is overly stressed, try to find out what the stressor is.

- *"I have fleas."* Fleas can make your cat itch. If she's allergic to flea saliva, they can make her absolutely miserable.

- *"Please help me relax."* If stress is the culprit, you can help make his life as stress-free as possible.

HOW TO SAY IT

- *Go to the veterinarian.* The source of your cat's problem could be fleas. It could be allergies. Or it could be something else, like feline hyperesthesia syndrome, a collection of symptoms of unknown origin that result in some compulsive behavior, including excessive grooming. In some instances, drug therapy can help. You need to rule out a physical reason for the excessive grooming before you try to handle it behaviorally.

- *Comb your cat with a flea comb over something white.* If you see black specs that become reddish brown when smeared with a moist finger, your cat has fleas. Even an indoor cat can get fleas, if he lives with animals who go outdoors. Consult your veterinarian for a solution to the problem. Once the fleas are gone, the compulsive grooming might vanish as well.

- *Try to pinpoint the source of the stress.* If your cat doesn't have a physical problem, then stress is probably the culprit. Remember that the excessive grooming is a symptom of stress, not the problem itself. Think about changes in your cat's environment, routine, or anything else that might cause her to be stressed. Then think about how you might alleviate that stress.

- *Give him some flower essences.* Green Hope Farm formulates flower essences for animals, including Healthy Coat, which can relieve itching. Anaflora offers Be Gone! to help rid pets of fleas or other parasites. Rescue Remedy might also help if stress is the culprit.

- *Provide stability for your cat.* Be extra careful about sticking to your daily routines, particularly mealtimes, to avoid stressing her. Make sure she has a safe place to eat and sleep (safe from kids or other pets).

- *Play with your cat.* Interactive play is a great way to relieve excess stress and energy. It's also good for your relationship with your cat, which adds to the stability in his life.

- *Train your cat.* Similarly, training provides mental stimulation, confidence, and bonding and is helpful for relieving stress. (See the chapter on clicker training for more information.)

- *Feed a high-quality diet.* Stress is hard on your cat's immune system. Good food strengthens her immune system. So it's especially important that your cat be fed a high-quality diet if she's under stress. Diet might also affect your cat's itchiness.

HOW NOT TO SAY IT

- *Don't punish or yell at your cat when he's grooming himself.* It's unlikely to make the compulsive behavior stop. In fact, it's likely to increase the behavior, since it will be stressful.

- *Don't rush to use drugs.* A veterinary behaviorist might be able to help your cat with drug therapy, but first, try to alleviate the source of the problem rather than addressing the symptom through drugs. Look for the culprit and address it.

chapter forty-two

Excessive Meowing

Leonard's Siamese cat, Ting, is a talker. With her distinctive meow, she lets Leonard know if she's upset, hungry, or just needing attention. Leonard doesn't mind her communicating, he just wishes it weren't so frequent and so loud!

They don't call it *cat*erwauling for nothing. Some cats are born talkers, and it can turn into a problem when the talking is incessant. By figuring out why your cat is spending so much time meowing, you can address the problem and end up with a more silent companion.

WHAT YOUR CAT IS TRYING TO TELL YOU

- *"I'm bored!"* Your cat might be meowing out of sheer boredom.

- *"Pay attention to me!"* Your cat might be making a bid for your attention.

- *"Don't leave me!"* Your cat's vocalizing after you leave the house might be a bid to get you to come back in.

- *"Hello, out there!"* Your cat might be trying to communicate with cats outdoors, particularly if she sees an intruder in her yard. If she's a female in heat, she might be trying to attract suitors.

- *"I'm in pain."* A cat will sometimes meow when she's sick or uncomfortable.

- *"I'm a talker."* Some cats are inherently more talkative. This is especially true of the Siamese and other Oriental breeds—it's in their genes.

HOW TO SAY IT

- *Spend more time with your cat.* Help stimulate him physically and mentally by spending quality time with him. Use interactive toys to help him practice being a predator. Groom him every day. Talk to him and pet him. This stimulation will help tire him out, which should make him want to nap rather than meow. And it should satisfy his desire for attention, which might be why he was meowing in the first place.

- *Enrich her environment.* If your cat spends hours at home alone, leave behind more things for her to do. Kitty condos, videos with birds in them, toys with treats inside will help alleviate boredom and perhaps curb the meowing.

- *Talk to your veterinarian.* If your usually silent cat starts meowing a lot, or if he vocalizes when you pick him up or touch him, he might be in pain or ill. (Increased vocalization and increased activity can be a sign of hyperthyroidism, which typically is seen in older cats.) Take him in for a checkup. Also, if your older cat starts meowing in the middle of the night, he may be disoriented in the dark house because his senses are on the decline. He may need you to call out to him so he can find you. If that's the case, installing a night-light might solve the problem.

- *Reward quiet behavior.* Feed, pet, groom, and play with your cat when she's being quiet. Teach her that good things come when she's not meowing. (It can be hard to remember to reward your cat when she's quiet, but it's worthwhile.)

- *Ignore obnoxious behavior.* If your cat is meowing to demand something, don't give it to him. Rather, turn your back on him until he's quiet—use earplugs or headphones if necessary—then reward him with what he's asking for, if you can.

- *Learn to read your cat's meows.* Your cat might be trying to tell you something. If you can differentiate between his "I'm frightened" and his "I'm hungry" or "Play with me" meows, then perhaps you'll appreciate the meowing as a form of communication rather than considering it excessive.

- *Spay or neuter.* If your cat is intact, he or she might be meowing out of sexual frustration or, in the case of females in heat, to attract suitors. Spaying or neutering will help take care of that problem. And it will reduce the risk of unwanted pregnancy in a world already full of unwanted cats.

- *Write it down.* Keep a log of when your cat is meowing excessively. Note the time and day and the circumstances surrounding the vocalizations. Then look for patterns that might help you identify the source of the problem.

- *Talk with a professional.* If you rule out a health reason for the inappropriate meowing, and nothing else is working, ask your vet for a referral to a veterinary behaviorist. He or she can help you pinpoint the reason for the meowing and address the problem at its source. Your written log will come in handy if you seek professional guidance.

- *Accept your cat for who he is.* Especially if your cat is a Siamese or other Oriental breed, he's going to meow. Try not to let it get on your nerves.

HOW NOT TO SAY IT

- *Don't reward the vocalizing.* If you respond every time your cat meows, you've taught him to vocalize when he wants something.

- *Don't wait for your cat to start vocalizing before giving her things that she desires.* If you anticipate her needs, she might not need to meow so much.

- *Don't scold your cat for meowing.* If your cat is vocalizing in order to get your attention, then any attention you give her—even if it's a scolding—rewards the vocalizing. Instead, ignore the behavior and reward quiet.

- *Don't give in.* If you're ignoring your cat's meowing, it will probably intensify. Don't give in to the pressure and give him attention (even negative attention) or food or any other reward. If you do, you're teaching him all he has to do is keep at it louder and longer. The problem may get worse before it gets better; you just have to hang tough and wait it out.

- *Don't expect too much.* Cats meow. Just like birds sing, people talk, and dogs bark. Don't expect your cat to be silent. Try to figure out what she's communicating to you and address her needs.

chapter forty-three

Fighting with other Cats

Jack and Penny's cats, Milo and Otis, can't seem to get along—or at least they only get along sometimes. Ever since Otis joined the family two years after Milo arrived, skirmishes break out. No one has been seriously hurt, but it's upsetting to all the family members (human and feline).

Cats aren't the pack animals that dogs are. They don't necessarily crave one another's company and territory is a big concern for them. Sometimes they try to resolve their issues through fighting. By trying to understand the reason for the fighting, and addressing those reasons, you might be able to resolve the problem. Keeping the cats separated when they can't be supervised is a must until the aggression can be worked out.

WHAT YOUR CAT IS TRYING TO TELL YOU

- *"Get out of my space!"* Sometimes forcing cats to share valuable real estate—like the litter box—can lead to aggression.

- *"I'm the boss around here."* Fighting can break out when one cat tries to improve his rank in the cats' pecking order.

- *"There's someone out there!"* Sometimes if a cat sees a perceived enemy he can't get to—like a neighborhood tomcat walking outside in his yard—he'll take it out on the closest cat.

- *"He's scaring me!"* If one cat bullies another, even if he's just teasing, the underdog might lash out in fear.

- *"We're just playing."* A feline wrestling match can sound to all the world like a fight.

HOW TO SAY IT

- *Look for reasons for uncharacteristic aggression.* Is your cat in pain? To the extent possible, examine her for any injuries. Use a muzzle and a towel if you need to keep yourself safe.

- *Provide ample litter boxes.* If your cats aren't getting along, something as simple as providing enough litter boxes so that they can keep out of each other's territory can help. A good rule of thumb is to have the same number of boxes as you have cats, plus one.

- *Give all your cats plenty of attention.* If hostilities start because a newcomer has entered the family, be sure to introduce the cats slowly. And don't neglect the resident cat or cats in your efforts to make the new cat feel at home.

- *Try to identify the source of the problem.* Is one cat picking on another, so that the trapped cat lashes out? Did your cats start fighting because they spied an enemy outside that they couldn't get to? Figuring out why your cats are fighting is the key to finding a solution to the problem.

- *Desensitize the cats toward each other.* If your cats aren't getting along, keep them separated and bring them together only under supervision. To start, bring one cat into the doorway of a room where an assistant is attending the other cat. Give treats to each cat for being in the presence of the other. Gradually, over the course of some days, bring the two closer together, all the while rewarding handsomely so that each cat recognizes that the other cat brings good things, not bad.

- *Play with your cats.* Help them blow off steam through (separate) interactive play with you.

- *Use Tellington TTouch.* Do gentle touches on each animal in separate rooms. Then, with a helper, work on both animals in the same room at the same time. This should help calm them and make them more comfortable with each other.

- *Try some Feliway.* This simulated feline facial pheromone can be very calming for cats. Use the Feliway diffuser in the rooms in which your fighting cats are staying. And spray it in the areas where your cats tend to fight.

- *Anticipate the fight and defuse the situation.* Know your cats' body language. When you see a twitching tail, or a scenario starting that is likely to turn into a fight, distract the aggressor with a toy and lure him away.

- *Feed separately.* If you have tensions between the cats in your house, you shouldn't free-feed: by doing so, you're giving one cat the opportunity to rule the food bowl. Instead, feed at scheduled times and feed the cats in separate rooms. Or feed them at a comfortable distance in the same room, with you supervising. Place the bowl a short distance away from the wall so that a cat feeling defensive can eat with his back to the wall and not worry about somebody sneaking up on him.

- *Invest in a cat tree.* According to feline behaviorist Pam Johnson-Bennett, author of *Think Like a Cat* among other works, a cat tree with multiple levels for cats to perch on can help keep the peace—and even allow cats who don't get along so well to peacefully coexist in the same room. Cats are more comfortable lying at an elevated level, where they have a good vantage point. Multiple levels will allow cats to keep their pecking order straight (with the top cat perched higher).

- *Know the difference between playing and fighting.* If it's a real fight, you'll hear lots of yowling and hissing. The fur will fly and you might see blood on one of your cats. In a fight, as opposed to a game, one cat is clearly the aggressor—in play, they switch offensive and defensive positions. If it's a fight, the cats will go out of their way to avoid each other when it's over. If they've just been playing, they'll go back to their normal behavior toward each other.

HOW NOT TO SAY IT

- *Don't try to break up the fight by picking up one of your cats.* You could get seriously injured. Instead, try to distract the combatants with a loud sound so that one has the opportunity to run away. Or toss something soft, like a blanket or pillow, on them or break up a fight by dowsing them with a glass of water. Once the fight is over, separate the cats for at least several hours. And supervise future interactions until you're sure that they're not ready to launch into another fight.

- *Don't punish a cat for fighting.* Punishment will leave your cat confused and potentially fearful. His trust in you will be damaged.

- *Don't just let the cats work things out.* Instead, intervene to remove the source of the conflict. Desensitize the cats to each other by very gradually bringing them together and rewarding calm behavior around each other.

- *Don't play favorites.* Even if it's clear to you that one cat is bullying another, both cats need your attention and affection. Keep the cats separated until you can trust them together. But don't fuss over the "victim" while giving the bully the silent treatment.

chapter forty-four

Finicky Eating

Melissa, a beautiful Scottish Fold, turns her nose up at food all the time. Her owner, Karen, gets frustrated because a food Melissa ate with gusto one day is scorned the next.

Cats need variety in their food. If you're feeding one type of food day in and day out, your cat might get sick of it and refuse to eat. It's dangerous for cats not to eat, so it's in the best interest of your cat to feed her a variety of foods. If she turns her nose up at something one day, give her something else that she will eat.

WHAT YOUR CAT IS TRYING TO TELL YOU

- *"I'm sick of this."* If you've been feeding your cat the same old food day after day, she may simply want (and need) a change.

- *"I eat one thing and one thing only."* If you try to introduce variety into your cat's diet after feeding a single food for a long period of time, he might not be willing to try something new. It's worth the effort to get him to eat a variety of foods.

- *"This tastes yucky."* Cats have individual tastes, just like we do. Even if you're feeding the same food you've always fed, the manufacturers may have made some changes, and the food might taste different to your cat.

- *"Where's the beef?"* Some commercial cat foods have higher-quality ingredients than others. If your cat turns up her nose at the cheapest foods, she isn't being a snob. She wants a diet that's meatier and more appropriate for her.

- *"I don't feel good."* If a cat who ordinarily eats well stops relishing his food, something might be wrong with him physically. He may have developed an intolerance to something in the food. Or he could be ill, have a sore mouth, or even a stuffy nose, which would prevent him from smelling the food.

HOW TO SAY IT

- *Give him variety.* Rotating flavors and even brands of food prevents your cat from becoming addicted to a single food. An added benefit: the food that was the mainstay of his diet might not be the perfect food for your particular cat. You can avoid nutritional deficiencies or excesses by switching his foods. In doing so, you expose your cat to a variety of flavors, making him less finicky.

- *Feed some real food.* Consider switching to a home-prepared diet, or a preprepared frozen fresh food. Some cats can be hard to switch over to a fresh-food diet, but others take to it from the start. Once the switch to fresh food is made, it's very easy to feed a varied diet. See the appendix for books on home feeding and sources for frozen raw diets.

- *Make the change slowly.* If your cat has a delicate digestive system, switch foods gradually, overlapping the two foods to avoid stomach upset.

- *Offer her something else.* If your cat turns her nose up at her food, offer her something different. You're not giving in to her finickiness. You're respecting her preferences.

- *Sweeten the deal.* If your cat is resisting a change in his diet, try making the new food more palatable by adding something especially flavorful. A little tuna juice poured on the new food might do the trick. Or you can buy a flavoring product made to entice pets to eat. Such products include Kitty Kaviar, which is made from dried fish, and Halo Dinner Party, made from meat and herbs, available at pet-supply stores and Web sites, as well as some health food stores.

- *Go to the vet.* If your cat suddenly stops eating—particularly if he's always eaten enthusiastically—take him to the vet. Sudden changes in eating habits could be a sign of real illness.

HOW NOT TO SAY IT

- *Don't stick to the same food, day after day.* Variety is the spice of life. And it's essential for optimum health.

- *Don't starve your cat until he eats what you've offered.* Not only is it unkind, it's dangerous: cats can develop life-threatening fatty liver disease (hepatic lipidosis) from not eating for just a few days. Even if your cat is overweight (especially if your cat is overweight), fasting can be dangerous.

- *Don't give him whatever he wants without regard for nutrition.* Sure, your cat would be thrilled with a diet of nothing but poached chicken breast or canned tuna. But that's not balanced nutrition. Either feed a commercial cat food he likes (switching types several times a year) or research a home-prepared diet and do it right.

- *Don't leave food out for your cat at all times.* The smell of food triggers a hunger response in cats, writes Anitra Frazier in *The New Natural Cat*. When you leave food out, your cat can smell it throughout the day. The trigger mechanism wears out, so to speak, and your cat doesn't feel hungry. If she's not hungry, she won't eat. And that can be dangerous.

chapter forty-five

Houseplant Eating

Before Denise adopted her cat, Rusty, her passion was her extensive collection of houseplants. She'd lovingly grown the plants for years and they were a major part of her home's decor. But the minute that frisky Rusty entered her home, he made a beeline for some of her favorite plants and started grazing on them. Denise yells at Rusty when he eats the plants, and has tried squirting him with water when he does it, but that only works until the next time he gets the urge to eat a plant. When she looks at her now-defoliated houseplants, Denise wants to cry.

Most cats enjoy eating plants. But not only is it hard on plants, it can also be hard on the cat, if the plant is toxic. A combination of providing your cat with his own healthy plants to eat, and keeping other plants out of reach, can solve the problem.

WHAT YOUR CAT IS TRYING TO TELL YOU

- *"Yummy."* Some plants taste good to cats.

- *"It feels good in my mouth."* Perhaps it's the feeling of the foliage between the teeth that gives the cat enjoyment.

- *"I need plants."* While cats are carnivores and require meat to thrive, plant material provides fiber that can aid in digestion.

- *"Why shouldn't I?"* If a plant is within easy reach of your cat and he has the urge to eat it, what's stopping him?

HOW TO SAY IT

- *Buy your cat her own plant.* Cats enjoy chewing on grass. And the grass is beneficial to their digestion. So if your cat doesn't have access to grass outdoors (or even if she does), buy or grow some cat grass. Grass species that are beneficial (and tasty!) to cats include oat, barley, and wheat grass. You can buy cat grass kits that include a mixture of seeds, as well as potting soil and, often, a pot. Pet-supply stores also sell already grown grass.

- *Grow some catnip for a special treat.* If your cat is a fan of dried catnip, he'll enjoy munching on the fresh herb. Keep it out of your cat's reach except on special occasions, though, or it will lose its power to create feline ecstasy.

- *Know which plants are toxic.* Be sure that none of the houseplants in your house is poisonous to your cat. See the "Feline Facts" at the end of this chapter for a partial list of poisonous plants, and the appendix for sources of more information. If you don't know the species of plants in your house, use the Internet or a book to help identify them.

- *Put away the valuable plants.* If you have plants you want to make sure your cat doesn't touch, don't let him anywhere near them. Create a cat-free room where your plants can thrive. (Keep any fresh catnip you're growing for your cat in this room and bring it out for special fun.)

- *Remove your cat when she eats the plants.* If you catch her chewing on a plant, calmly pick her up and take her to her own grass. Praise her for paying attention to the sanctioned grass.

- *Hang plants so that your cat can't get to them.* A plant hanging from the ceiling should be out of reach from your cat's teeth. But don't let dangling fronds be a temptation. Trim hanging plants so they are well out of your cat's reach.

Toxic Plants

According to the ASPCA Animal Poison Control Center, some common houseplants that are poisonous to cats include:

Plants that affect the heart:

Convallaria majalis—lily of the valley

Nerium oleander—oleander

Rhododendron species—rhododendron, azalea, and rosebay

Taxus species—American, Japanese, English, and western yew

Digitalis purpurea—foxglove

Kalanchoe species—kalanchoe

Plants that could cause kidney failure:

Certain species of lilies

Rhubarb (*Rheum species*)—leaves only

Plants that could cause liver failure:

Cycads (*Cycad* species)

Mushroom (*Amanita phalloides*)

Plants that could cause multiple effects:

Autumn crocus (*Colchicum* species)—bloody diarrhea, renal, liver damage, and bone marrow suppression

Castor bean (*Ricinus* species)—can cause renal failure, convulsions, and death

■ *Wash any plants you bring home.* Even if the plant species is nontoxic, the nursery could have sprayed it with pesticide.

■ *Know the signs that your cat has eaten a poisonous plant.* Depending on the plant, the symptoms may include salivation, vomiting, bloody diarrhea, difficulty breathing, fever, abdominal pain, depression, collapse, trembling, irregular heartbeat, and sores in the mouth or throat. If you see these signs and suspect your cat has ingested a plant, call your veterinarian or the ASPCA's Animal Poison Control Center at 888-426-4435. If you know the species of plant eaten, be sure to tell the person you speak with.

HOW NOT TO SAY IT

- *Don't take any chances on toxic plants.* If you're not sure whether a plant in your house is toxic, contact a local botanical garden or state extension service for help in identifying it.

- *Don't punish your cat for eating the plants.* While it might make you feel better to yell at him for munching on your plant, it won't have a lasting effect. Squirting might get him to run away from the plant at that moment. But picking him up and calmly taking him to his own plant gets him away from the plant while also redirecting him to appropriate behavior. Removing inappropriate plants takes care of the problem. And these tactics don't have a negative effect on your relationship.

chapter forty-six

Hunting

One day her cat, Joe, brought Marilyn a toy mouse and dropped it at her feet for her to throw for him. At least Marilyn thought it was a toy mouse. When she reached down to pick it up to start the game, she discovered, to her horror, that it was a real mouse that Joe had recently killed!

Many cat owners are horrified that their cats hunt. They worry about the effect of their cat's hunting on the wildlife. They worry about the potential ill effects that eating their prey could have on their cats. And they hate it when their cats bring their kills inside. If you're worried about your cat's hunting, the easiest solution is to not let him outside.

WHAT YOUR CAT IS TRYING TO TELL YOU

- *"What do you expect? I'm a cat."* Hunting is what cats do. If you give your cat the opportunity to hunt, he'll probably hunt.

- *"It's not going to hurt me."* The most natural diet for a cat is freshly killed prey. Unless the prey has been eating poison, your cat's supplementing his diet with prey shouldn't be a problem.

- *"Give me something else to do."* By playing with your cat, you can provide outlets for his hunting instincts.

HOW TO SAY IT

- *Keep your cat inside.* If your cat hunts and it bothers you, don't give him access to prey. Instead, play with him using faux prey, like feather toys, to exercise his hunting instincts. See the chapter on converting an outdoor cat into an indoor cat for tips on making this transition.

- *Bell your cat.* If you feel you can't keep your cat inside, try adding a bell to his collar to warn prey of his approach. Your stealthy cat may well learn to stalk without ringing the bell, but it's worth a try.

- *Play with your cat.* Use interactive toys to simulate hunting (see the chapter on playing) and keep him inside. That should not only stop him from killing animals, it should also satisfy the hunter within him.

- *Decide not to worry about it.* If the only concern you have about your cat being outdoors is his hunting (there are plenty of other concerns you should have about your outdoor cat), try to let go of it. The issue of cats' impact on songbird and rodent populations is a controversial one—some people say the impact is severe, others claim it is minimal. If your cat is supplementing his diet with fresh food, more power to him.

HOW NOT TO SAY IT

- *Don't allow your cat access to prey.* It's as simple as that. Keeping your cat inside will eliminate his ability to hunt wild prey, unless mice are living inside your house. In that case, you might be grateful for his assistance.

- *Don't use mouse poison.* If you have mice that you want to rid your house of, your cat may take care of the problem. Don't supplement his efforts with mouse poison, though. If he eats a poisoned mouse, he could become poisoned himself.

- *Don't be so squeamish.* If your only problem with your cat's hunting is that he brings in his kill (and doesn't eat it), just dispose of it like you would other disgusting pet-related things, like poop. Put a plastic bag over your hand like a glove, grab the offending carcass, turn the bag inside out over it, and dispose of it, bag and all.

chapter forty-seven

Kneading Your Lap

When Simba hops on the lap of his owner, Louise, he frequently starts kneading the fabric, by lifting first one foot, then the other, alternately extending and retracting his claws. He usually purrs and sometimes he even drools a little while he's doing it. This wouldn't be a problem, except that Simba's long nails become caught in the fabric and sometimes even hurt Louise's skin.

It's actually a great compliment—a sign of love—when your cat kneads you. Kittens do this to their mothers when they're nursing to help stimulate the flow of milk. When they do it after they're weaned, they're harkening back to the contentment of kittenhood. If your cat's claws catch when she kneads, then simply keep her claws shorter.

WHAT YOUR CAT IS TRYING TO TELL YOU

- *"I love you."* By kneading you, your cat is treating you like her mother. Think of it as a feline valentine.

- *"I feel safe and happy."* A nursing kitten must feel about as warm and safe as a being can be. By kneading you and reliving his time nursing his mother, your cat is showing you that he trusts you and feels very safe.

HOW TO SAY IT

- *Trim his nails.* If your cat's kneading is painful, or if you're worried he'll ruin the fabric he's kneading, just keep his nails shorter. See the chapter on nail trimming for information on the procedure.

- *Cover your legs.* Keep a lap robe handy and cover your legs when you see your cat heading for your lap. That'll blunt any pain associated with the kneading.

- *Tell your cat you love her.* Return this display of affection with one of your own. Tell your cat you love her and show her by caressing her as she sits in your lap. Blink your eyes slowly at her.

HOW NOT TO SAY IT

- *Don't ask your cat not to knead.* It's such a natural action that it's difficult, if not impossible, to train it out of your cat. You might as well ask him not to purr!

- *Don't throw your cat off your lap when she's kneading.* If she happens to be doing it at an inconvenient time for you, gently pick your cat up and place her on the ground. If the only reason you don't want her to knead is that it hurts you, keep her nails shorter or cover your lap. Try to enjoy this expression of love and trust.

chapter forty-eight

Not Using the Litter Box

Bonnie's cat, Samantha, was always fastidious about using the litter box. But Bonnie started finding nasty surprises—cat urine in the laundry basket and feces in the potted plants. Why had Samantha suddenly changed her litter-box habits?

It can take a little detective work to figure out why a cat will stop using the litter box, but if you look hard enough, you can find a reason. And with a little retraining (either of you or your cat—or perhaps both of you) this very common problem can be solved.

WHAT YOUR CAT IS TRYING TO TELL YOU

- *"I don't feel well."* Medical problems can cause cats to be unable to hold their urine or feces. Or they can cause pain upon elimination, which the cat soon learns to associate with the litter box, making her want to avoid it.

- *"The litter box needs cleaning."* One of the reasons we like cats so much is their clean nature. Like you, your cat doesn't want to use a dirty toilet.

- *"I don't like the litter."* Even a meticulously kept litter box can be distasteful to a cat. The litter may be too rough for sensitive paws (particularly in declawed cats), it may smell funny, or it may be too deep or too shallow.

- *"The location is wrong."* Cats won't use a litter box that is too close to their food or one that leaves them feeling vulnerable.

- *"I'm stressed."* Sometimes cats will eliminate outside the box when they are stressed about something.

- *"This is my territory."* Territorial marking, which you'll usually see on vertical surfaces, requires different strategies than inappropriate elimination. (See the chapter on spraying.)

HOW TO SAY IT

- *Take your cat to the veterinarian to rule out any health problems.* If there's a medical reason for the inappropriate elimination, it does no good to try to treat it behaviorally without addressing the health issue. Such problems could include a urinary tract infection, an endocrine problem like diabetes, constipation, infectious or noninfectious diseases, or side effects of medication.

- *Take a step back and reevaluate the location of the litter box.* Was it put there for your convenience or the cat's? Your cat's preference is really the one that matters. If the litter box is tucked away in the corner, he might feel he can't use it while keeping an eye out for any disturbances. If it is off the beaten path, it might not be convenient for you to scoop regularly. Is it too near your cat's food? Since cat urine is so strong smelling, it sends a clear message to predators. Cats instinctively keep their nest (their food, water, and bed) away from potential predators—so they don't want their urine smell to be anywhere near it. Make sure your litter box is in a location that your cat is comfortable using.

- *Do a little detective work.* Take a look at where your cat is choosing to eliminate. Does it provide any clues about her preferences? If she's going in the houseplants, perhaps she would prefer a softer, more soil-like litter. If she's going on bare floors, try leaving a portion of the litter box bare (with litter at the other end for covering). If she is going to the bathroom under the desk, maybe she'd prefer a covered litter box.

- *Clean all areas your cat has used inappropriately.* Use an enzymatic cleaner to completely eliminate, not just mask, the odor. Cats tend to potty where they've soiled or urinated before. Remove the scent to discourage the repeat bathroom visit to the area. After cleaning, you can place your cat's food on top of the area; he won't want to potty where he eats. After the problem is solved, you'll be able to move those food bowls.

- *Pull up your sleeves and clean the litter box.* Or get a new one. Even if you do buy a new one, be sure to give it a good scrubbing before filling it with litter. Cats have a much keener sense of smell than humans. So even if the box seems odor-free to you, it might be offensive to your cat. You should clean your cat's litter box by scooping out wet clumps and feces once a day, if not more often. Anitra Frazier, author of *The New Natural Cat,* suggests that you keep the litter box in the bathroom and "flush" it every time you flush your own toilet. Remember, if the smell is bad enough to be offensive to you, it's bound to be much worse for your cat.

- *Give a self-scooping litter box a try.* If you find you are not able to scoop the box as often as your cat would like, an automated box, like the Littermaid or the Litter Robot, might solve the problem. They automatically put the clumps into a covered waste area a few minutes after your cat leaves the box.

- *Get more litter boxes.* If you have a multicat household or a multilevel house, you may need more litter boxes. A good rule of thumb is to have one for each cat in the household plus one. Shared boxes fill up fast. Even if you have only one cat, an extra litter box might solve your problem. Some cats prefer separate boxes for urination and defecation. Also, if you have older cats, or any with mobility problems, provide a litter box on each floor of the house.

- *Try a different litter.* If you're using a regular clay litter, give the clumping type a try. Or try a different depth. But remember to keep close track while you're experimenting so that you can figure out the exact combination that works best for your cat.

- *Think about stressors.* Have there been any changes in your cat's environment? New family members? New furniture? See if you can pinpoint the stressor and address it. Stress can cause inappropriate elimination.

- *Do TTouch to help alleviate stress.* Regular TTouch sessions should soothe both of you.

- *Make houseplants less attractive as toilets.* If your cat is using the soil of houseplants as a litter box, try putting some big rocks in the pot. Or, if possible, cover the top of the pot with some hardware cloth or mesh, with a hole cut out for the plant stem. Most important, listen to what your cat is telling you: she wants some soft, soil-like litter. If the litter in her box is clay litter or some type of pellets, try some softer, scoopable litter.

HOW NOT TO SAY IT

- *Don't rub your cat's nose in his mistake.* Under no circumstances should you punish your cat while he's eliminating or after he's finished. This will teach him nothing more than to hide while he eliminates and to be scared of you. Besides, rubbing a cat's sensitive nose in urine or feces is cruel.

- *Don't pick her up while she's eliminating and take her to the litter box.* Again, this causes negative associations with the act of eliminating—and with the litter box. Your cat will learn not to eliminate when you're around and, worse, to find a hiding place to do it in.

- *Don't use deodorizing litter.* It's made for you, not for your cat. It might mask the smell to you, but your cat will probably be as offended by the deodorants as he was by the litter box smell. Clean the litter more often instead.

- *Don't wait for the litter box to smell bad before cleaning it.* Keep it fresh by cleaning it at least once a day, and neither you nor your cat will have to deal with an unpleasant smell.

- *Don't place the litter box near an appliance that makes noise.* Your cat might be startled while eliminating and develop a fear of the litter box.

- *Don't put off cleaning the litter box because it's such an ugly chore.* Doing it more frequently will make the job easier. And it will keep your cat happier. Wouldn't you rather clean up a litter box than a mess on the carpet?

- *Don't confuse a litter-box problem with spraying.* If your cat is spraying to mark his territory (backing up to something, lifting his tail, and spraying, usually while his tail twitches), you address that problem differently. See the chapter on spraying.

chapter forty-nine

Shyness

Kendra's two cats, Mickey and Penny, are as different as night and day. Mickey is outgoing and loves nothing more than to jump into the lap of any visitors. Penny is shy and stays under the bed when any non–family members are in the house. It even took her several weeks to warm up to Kendra when she was adopted.

Cats are individuals. There's nothing wrong with being shy, provided the shy cat is happy. There are a few things you can do to try to build your shy cat's confidence, but you should also respect your cat for who she is.

WHAT YOUR CAT IS TRYING TO TELL YOU

- *"I'm happiest under here, thank you."* A cat who is perfectly outgoing with family members can shoot under the bed the minute the doorbell rings. If that's where he feels safe, that's okay.

- *"I just need some TLC."* If your shy cat is new to your family, she may just need to feel loved and secure before coming out of her shell.

- *"I'm stressed."* If your normally shy and retiring cat has stopped interacting altogether, look for stressors in his environment and try to address them.

- *"I don't feel good."* It might be illness, not shyness, that's keeping your cat from interacting with you.

HOW TO SAY IT

- *Play with your cat.* Interactive toys can help him gain confidence as he exercises his natural predatory instincts. But you might need to tone your game down at first—your shy cat might not be up for raucous play. Even if he is under the bed, you can still quietly play with him by dangling a toy off the edge of the bed so he can see it from beneath and bat at it.

- *Clicker train your cat.* Training helps build confidence as she figures out how to get you to click and reward her. Clicker training is fun for both of you and provides some quality time together. See the chapter on clicker training for more information.

- *Be patient.* Your cat needs to become comfortable at her own pace—not yours.

- *Try a flower essence.* Calm Kitty formula and Columbine from Anaflora, as well as the Bach Flower Remedy Larch, can help shyness. Put some in your cat's water to help him feel more comfortable with his surroundings.

- *Give your cat places to hide out in the open.* Put a soft-sided cat tunnel or even a paper bag or cardboard box in the room where you'd like her to spend time with you. This will help her feel less exposed.

- *Put a little T-shirt on him.* Tellington TTouch practitioners advise that T-shirts can provide a feeling of security for animals. Tiny T-shirts made for premature babies can fit a cat well (certainly larger T-shirts would work for larger cats). Put the shirt on your cat with the tag in the front. If your cat freezes or it affects his movement, take it off after just a few minutes. If he's comfortable wearing it, keep it on as long as he tolerates it. If you think the T-shirt is making him feel braver, and he's comfortable in it, you could put it on before stressful situations, like going to the veterinarian or receiving visitors (though don't let them laugh at your cat!).

■ *Try some Tellington TTouches.* Unless your cat is so shy she won't allow you to touch her at all, do circular touches and ear touches daily to help calm her and build your bond.

■ *Look for stressors.* Your cat might be stressed out, not just naturally shy. Think about any changes that you might have made to his environment. Have you done renovations or added carpeting? Added any pets to your household? Try to address the stressors (make sure your cat has a safe room, away from the stressors, and has an elevated place to go to get away from dogs, for example) and he might become more outgoing.

■ *Take your cat to the veterinarian if her shyness is new.* If your once-outgoing cat becomes shy, or your shy cat withdraws entirely, she may be ill or in pain. Take her to the veterinarian to see if there is a medical explanation for the change in behavior.

HOW NOT TO SAY IT

■ *Don't force yourself on your cat.* Let him come to you. Then gently stroke him and talk to him when he does. But don't push him past his limits.

■ *Don't force your cat to interact with others.* As long as your cat is happy, she should be able to stay in a safe place if she's feeling shy. Let her come out at her own pace.

■ *Don't tower over your cat.* And don't rush at him. Crouch down to his level and let him approach you. Use this body language to communicate that you're gentle and to be trusted.

■ *Don't lose your patience.* You didn't adopt a cat so that you could feed an animal you never see. But over time, if you treat her gently, patiently, and with kindness, she'll begin to trust you. Losing your patience with your shy cat will only alienate her further.

chapter fifty

Spraying

Eric and Mary's cat, Buster, has made a mess of their once-pristine house. The unneutered male marks their territory by spraying inside the house whenever he sees a cat in his yard. The furniture and walls are marred and the smell is terrible. The couple has considered banishing Buster to the outdoors because they can't take it anymore!

Anyone who has been exposed to cat spray—particularly from intact males—knows that the stench is almost unbearable. And it's difficult to get rid of. But stopping your cat from spraying isn't impossible. It just takes some behavior modification, consistency, and neutering, if that hasn't been done already.

WHAT YOUR CAT IS TRYING TO TELL YOU

- *"This is my territory!"* Urine is one of the ways that cats mark their territory.

- *"There are too many cats here."* Sometimes adding another cat to your family can upset the equilibrium and prompt a resident cat to start spraying.

- *"What are you doing in my yard?!"* An indoor cat might start spraying when he sees a cat (or other animal) in his yard.

- *"I'm stressed."* Moving to a new home, adding a new human family member to the household, a change in the family structure as a result of death or divorce or someone moving out, renovating your house . . . all these can trigger spraying.

- *"I'm a man."* Some intact male cats will start spraying when they reach sexual maturity.

- *"What's this new thing? I'd better mark it."* If you add new furniture or new carpeting to your house, your cat may feel the need to include it in his territory by marking it.

HOW TO SAY IT

- *An ounce of prevention.* Spay or neuter your cat *before* they start marking their territory by spraying.

- *Spay or neuter.* If your spraying cat is intact, take him or her to the vet pronto to be sterilized. While spraying is common for unneutered males and females in heat, only 10 percent of neutered males and 5 percent of spayed females spray frequently, according to a 1984 study by B. L. Hart and L. Cooper. The age at which the cats were neutered and spayed did not seem to have a bearing on spraying.

- *Get a vet check.* As with the onset of any new behavior, it's a good idea to have your cat looked over by a veterinarian to rule out any physical reason for the problem.

- *Make sure it's spraying, not a litter-box problem.* If he's standing up, tail erect and quivering, releasing small amounts of urine onto a vertical surface, that's spraying. If he's squatting and leaving large amounts of urine outside the box, that's a litter-box problem that you will tackle differently. (See the chapter on not using the litter box.)

- *Clean your house thoroughly.* You want to remove all traces of cat urine. Use an enzymatic cleaner in order to remove rather than merely mask the odor. Do this before starting a behavior modification program and as soon as possible after your cat sprays. If you're planning to use Feliway, clean with plain water only.

- *Try some Feliway.* This simulated feline facial pheromone can be very helpful for spraying. Cats rub their cheeks on objects to mark them. But they don't spray where they've rubbed their cheeks. The simulated facial hormone will discourage them from spraying. It's also calming. It comes in two forms: a spray, which you can spritz right on the area that has been marked (after cleaning up the urine with water), once or twice a day for a month. You can also spray it—at cat-nose height—on vertical objects that he might be interested in marking. The other form is a room diffuser, which plugs into an outlet and diffuses the harmless and odorless substance continuously. Use it in the room where your cat has sprayed. If he has sprayed in more than one room, use another diffuser in one of the additional rooms. The diffuser lasts thirty days.

- *Reduce the stress in your cat's life.* For many cats, spraying is a reaction to stress or excitement. Do your best to keep things on an even keel; make sure your cat's meals are served at the scheduled time, for example. Play with your cat to reduce tension and burn off excess energy.

- *Consult with an animal communicator.* A session with a communicator could reveal the motivation for the spraying, which you could address. It could also give you the opportunity to explain to your cat why the spraying is such a problem for you. Sometimes, through a communicator, you can arrive at a solution or a compromise that takes care of the problem.

- *Try some flower essences.* Anaflora has a special Spraying Cat Formula that can be helpful. Rescue Remedy, a Bach Flower Remedy, can help your cat cope with stress.

- *Play with him in the areas in which he's spraying.* If your cat is marking because he's stressed, you can change the way he feels about those areas of the house where he's marking by playing with him there.

- *Keep track of the spraying behavior.* By writing down when and where your cat sprays, you can identify the triggers and work to eliminate them.

- *Take him away from the window.* If your cat is spraying because he sees other cats in his yard, block access to the window that overlooks the offending yard or try asking your neighbors to keep their cats indoors. Tell them about the health benefits to the cats if they're kept inside.

- *Separate the offenders.* If the spraying in your household is a war between more than one cat—or if one cat is spraying because of the presence of another one—keep them separated until they calm down, then use treats (and a clicker, if you clicker train your cat) to change the cats' associations with each other from negative to positive. Gradually reintroduce them by bringing something that smells like one of the cats (his bed or a special toy) to the spraying cat and giving him treats in the presence of the other cat's smell. Then bring the actual cat in, keeping him within sight, but at a distance from the spraying cat. Treat the sprayer nonstop for five to ten seconds, then remove the other cat. Repeat until you can bring the cat in closer to the sprayer.

- *Talk to your veterinarian about possible solutions.* A holistic vet might be able to suggest some calming herbs. A conventional vet might give you a prescription. A veterinary behaviorist can custom-design a behavior modification plan.

- *Have cats of the same gender.* Male cats (even neutered ones) spray more when they live with female cats. Female cats don't differentiate that way in their spraying. Next time you're considering adding your cat to a family, you might keep this in mind.

HOW NOT TO SAY IT

- *Don't treat spraying like a litter-box problem.* If your cat is lifting his or her tail and spraying onto a vertical surface, tail aquiver, it's more than inappropriate elimination. The solutions suggested for litter-box problems don't apply here.

- *Don't turn your cat out.* Try to resolve the problem, using the techniques described on the previous pages, before your turn your cat into an outdoor cat.

- *Don't punish your cat for spraying.* Punishment for this very natural behavior isn't going to be effective. Some forms, like rubbing the cat's nose in the urine or hitting him, are actually cruel. Punishing your cat will increase his stress, which might make the problem even worse.

- *Don't rush to drug.* Pharmaceutical therapy should be one of the last options you explore. You don't want to risk side effects.

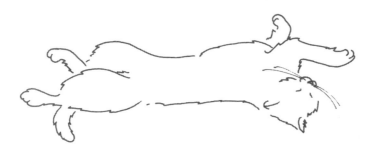

chapter fifty-one

Trash-Can Raiding

Mozart loves nothing more than to climb into the kitchen trash can and chow down on whatever he can find in there. His owner, Jane, has come home to find the trash can knocked over onto its side, its contents spilled all over, and the remnants of some chicken bones left behind as evidence of his feasting.

Some cats like to help themselves to the trash. It's very difficult to train them to stay away from the trash when going into it is so innately rewarding. But there is an easy solution to the problem: don't leave the trash can where your cat can get it.

WHAT YOUR CAT IS TRYING TO TELL YOU

- *"This stuff tastes good!"* Trash cans are often full of stuff that tastes great to cats. Unfortunately, some of that stuff, like cooked chicken bones or foil, can be dangerous to them. But they don't care—it tastes good.

- *"I like a challenge!"* Some curious cats enjoy using their paws to open the lids of trash cans. It might take a little ingenuity on your part to make the trash raid-proof.

- *"Why shouldn't I?"* Trash-can raiding is rewarding for your cat. If the basket's just sitting there, what's to stop her from taking advantage of the situation?

- *Put away the trash.* It couldn't be more simple. Don't leave it out for your cat to get into. If this means taking out the kitchen trash every single day, so be it. Stash the trash under the sink. Put the bathroom trash in the linen closet or inside the shower stall. Do what you have to do. If you have a trash raider, don't tempt him!

- *Try bungee cords.* If for some reason you can't get your trash out of your cat's reach, use a can with a lid and try using bungee cords to keep the lid on tight.

- *Give your cat plenty of exercise.* If she's tired out from interactive play by the time you go to work, she might snooze rather than explore.

- *Leave your cat toys that will keep him occupied.* Toys with holes into which you can stuff treats that fall out when he bats it around might be a good substitute for getting into mischief.

- *Train your cat.* It might be the mental stimulation of figuring out how to get into the trash that attracts her to that forbidden territory. With daily clicker-training sessions, your cat will get the mental stimulation she craves—and perhaps leave the trash alone.

- *Don't leave attractive things in the trash.* Take those chicken bones or empty tuna cans outside to the trash bins rather than tempting your cat by leaving them in the kitchen trash. Even the most well-behaved cat might find that to be too much temptation!

- *Don't booby-trap your trash.* It makes it a hassle for you to throw things away, and it's unfair punishment when you can just put the trash out of the cat's reach.

- *Don't punish the cat for your own error.* If you've left the trash out for him to get to, it's your own fault.

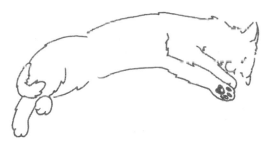

chapter fifty-two

Waking You Up at Night

Robin's tabby cat, Pete, is a hellion at night. He sleeps all day while she is at work, and when the lights go out, he doesn't sleep for long. He may be able to amuse himself quietly, but long about four or five in the morning he starts trying to wake Robin up. He'll pat her face, even playfully bite at her toes, and when all else fails he just starts meowing. Robin has found that if she feeds Pete when he wakes her up, he'll go back to sleep for at least an hour or two. But she doesn't appreciate having her sleep disrupted!

Cats are nocturnal by nature and in the wild they hunt during predawn hours. For housecats, that translates into a desire to play—and eat—in the wee hours of the morning. Unfortunately, this is usually in conflict with the human's sleep schedule. If you help your cat get on your schedule by playing with him, then feeding him at bedtime, and if you don't reward him for awakening you, eventually he might let you sleep the whole night through.

WHAT YOUR CAT IS TRYING TO TELL YOU

■ *"I'm awake, why aren't you?"* Cats are nocturnal and they're social creatures, so when they're ready for some fun at night, they want your company.

■ *"I'm hungry!"* If your cat's eating schedule is such that she's hungry in the middle of the night, she'll let you know.

■ *"I'm just having a little fun."* Whether your cat wakes you up for a play session or plays with his toys on his own, he'll probably be noisy about it.

HOW TO SAY IT

■ *Change his feeding schedule.* If the main reason your cat seems to wake you up is to eat, change his feeding schedule so that he gets a meal before bed. If you usually leave food down for him all the time, take it up in the evening, and fill the bowl with fresh food at bedtime.

■ *Play with your cat at bedtime.* A rousing game with an interactive toy, followed by a meal, might get her to sleep through the night. It mimics a wild cat's eating schedule: hunt, then eat, then nap. If your cat is getting more exercise, she'll need more sleep. And she'll stay healthier.

■ *Ignore your cat's attempts to wake you.* If you don't ignore him, you reward his attention-getting behavior, which will cause it to be repeated. And if you hold out for a long time, then give in, you're only making matters worse. You'll teach your cat that if he caterwauls long enough, he'll get results.

■ *Provide some toys that your cat can enjoy on her own.* The Cat Dancer, which dangles little pieces of cardboard from a flexible wire, can be attached to a wall (and detached for interactive use). The Panic Mouse, a battery-operated toy, swings a "mouse" around at the end of a wire and uses unpredictable motions. There are glow-in-the-dark balls available as well as battery-operated balls that light up when touched. You can also buy hollow balls with a hole in them. Put treats or food in the hole and the food dribbles out the toy when your cat bats it around. Any of these toys could cause a little commotion, so you'll want to put them far from your bedroom if you don't want to be awakened. None of these toys should replace your interactive play sessions, which are important for your relationship with your cat, but they can keep her occupied when you're asleep.

- *Evict your cat from your bedroom.* If you can put your cat in another part of the house, he can play all he wants in the middle of the night. For many cat lovers, this is a last resort. But if it comes down to sleep deprivation or sleeping with your cat, separate bedrooms might win out. Just be sure that your cat gets some prebedtime snuggling time with you. And make sure his nighttime area has plenty of things to do. A window through which he can watch the night's activities (flying insects and so forth) can provide a pleasant diversion.

- *Talk with your vet if your older cat suddenly starts being very active or vocal at night.* These can be signs of an overactive thyroid gland, which should be addressed medically or surgically.

HOW NOT TO SAY IT

- *Don't give in to her attempts to wake you up.* If you feed your cat when she wakes you up in the middle of the night, she'll do it every night because you've rewarded the behavior. If she just wants your attention, or a pat on the head, giving her any kind of attention or affection might quiet her, but it rewards the behavior. Your best bet is to try to ignore the behavior (or isolate the cat if you have to).

- *Don't punish your cat for waking you up by trying to trap him under the blankets, yelling at him, swatting him, or making a loud noise.* He might just start trying to get your attention by meowing from a distance. And it's not good for your relationship with your cat.

chapter fifty-three

Walking on the Counter

It drives Mike crazy when his cat, Minnie, jumps up and walks on the counter. He's always finding cat hair in his butter and even in the silverware drawer. She jumps off when he yells at her and runs toward her, but it doesn't stop her from getting up the next time she has the inclination.

Cats are accustomed to walking wherever they want. They're so agile that jumping up on the counter takes virtually no effort. And, of course, the counter is full of potentially interesting items. If your cat walks on the counter you have a few choices: don't give her access to the counter, reward her for staying off the counter, or stop worrying about it.

WHAT YOUR CAT IS TRYING TO TELL YOU

- *"What's up there?"* You know what they say about cats and curiosity. Since food is often on the counter, many cats want to jump up there and check things out.

- *"What do you expect?"* Cats tend to walk wherever they want. And they like high places. There's often food up there. Counters are cat magnets.

- *Eliminate access.* Close your kitchen door when you're not in the kitchen.

- *Reward your cat for good behavior.* When your cat stays on the floor or sits elsewhere in the kitchen, toss her a tidbit and praise her.

- *Get over it.* Don't leave anything dangerous on the counter (like knives) and don't leave out food you don't want your cat getting into. Then try not to get too upset about this behavior. It tends to go with the territory of having a cat.

- *Clicker train your cat to go to his place while you're working at the counter.* Sound impossible? In *Getting Started: Clicker Training for Cats,* Karen Pryor offers step-by-step instructions.

HOW NOT TO SAY IT

- *Don't punish your cat for counter walking.* Common forms of punishment include spraying water at your cat, yelling, setting off an air horn, swatting him, and unceremoniously dumping him off the counter. Punishment isn't effective. Nor is it fair, especially if you're doing it after the fact.

- *Don't use aversiveness.* Some people recommend ways to booby-trap your counter to scare your cat off—covered mousetraps, pyramids of cans to tumble on his head, even mats that provide a shock when touched by paws. Why give your cat a nasty surprise for doing something natural when you can manage the situation by closing off the kitchen?

Appendix

Resources for Further Information

GENERAL CAT CARE
Books

Christensen, Wendy, and the Staff of the Humane Society of the United States. *The Humane Society of the United States Complete Guide to Cat Care*. New York: St. Martin's Press, 2002.

Church, Christine. *Housecat: How to Keep Your Indoor Cat Sane and Sound*. New York: Howell Book House, 1998.

Frazier, Anitra, with Norma Eckroate. *The New Natural Cat: A Complete Guide for Finicky Owners,* newly revised and expanded. New York: Penguin, 1990.

Johnson-Bennett, Pam. *Think Like a Cat: How to Raise a Well-Adjusted Cat Not a Sour Puss*. New York: Penguin Books, 2000.

Shojai, Amy D. *Complete Kitten Care*. New York: New American Library, 2002.

Spadafori, Gina, and Paul D. Pion, DVM, DACVIM. *Cats for Dummies*, 2nd ed. Foster City, Calif.: IDG Books Worldwide, 2000.

The Whole Cat Journal
P.O. Box 1337
Radford, VA 24143-1337
540-763-2925
www.wholecat.com

The Whole Cat Journal provides information on holistic health and nutrition issues, positive means of dealing with problems, and extensive product reviews.

BABIES AND CHILDREN
Crib Safety Nets
Web Marketing Partners
353 Lafayette Street
Salem, MA 01970
888-688-7728
http://www.ezcom.com/tots.htm

Safety Matters™
478 Barberry Road
Highland Park, IL 60035
800-972-3306
info@safetymatters.com
www.safetymatters.com

DESENSITIZING COMPACT DISC
Sound Sensibilities CDs for noise desensitization. This audio CD contains forty to fifty minutes of the sound of babies crying. $17.95. Available from:

Hanalei Pets, Inc.
P.O. Box 697
Carlsborg, WA 98324
888-876-9364
Outside U.S.: 360-683-9646
Fax: 360-683-5755
www.hanaleipets.com

BEHAVIOR AND TRAINING
Books
Ackerman, DVM, Lowell. *Cat Behavior and Training: Veterinary Advice for Owners.* Neptune City, N.J.: TFH, 1996.

Anderson, Karen. *Why Cats Do That: A Collection of Curious Kitty Quirks.* Minocqua, Wisc.: Willow Creek Press, 2001.

Bessant, Claire. *How to Talk to Your Cat.* London: Smith Gryphon, Ltd., 1992. U.S. ed.: New York: Barron's, 1993.

Budiansky, Stephen. *The Character of Cats: The Origins, Intelligence, Behavior, and Stratagems of Felis silvestris catus.* New York: Viking, 2002.

Johnson-Bennett, Pam. *Hiss and Tell: True Stories from the Files of a Cat Shrink.* New York: Penguin, 1996.

Johnson-Bennett, Pam. *Psycho Kitty? Understanding Your Cat's "Crazy" Behavior.* Freedom, Calif.: The Crossing Press, 1998.

Pryor, Karen. *Getting Started: Clicker Training for Cats.* Waltham, Mass.: Sunshine Books, 2001.

Wood, Deborah. *The Tao of Meow: Understanding and Training Your Cat the Taoist Way.* New York: Dell, 1999.

Video

Clicker Magic: The Art of Clicker Training, Karen Pryor, 1997.

Other resources

Karen Pryor's company (for information, books, clickers, other training equipment):

Sunshine Books, Inc.
49 River Street, Suite 3
Waltham, MA 02453
800-472-5425
www.clickertraining.com

Cat-Clicker yahoogroup
http://groups.yahoo.com/group/Cat-Clicker/
Cat-Clicker-subscribe@yahoogroups.com

Sources for great cat treats, toys and other accessories:
www.petextras.com
www.sitstay.com
www.cattoys.com

Feliway simulated feline facial pheromone:
Farnam Pet Products
Phoenix, AZ 85067
800-234-2269
www.farnampet.com
Feliway is available through veterinarians and major pet-supply stores.

DEATH AND GRIEVING
Books

Anderson, Moira. *Coping with the Sorrow on the Loss of Your Pet.* Loveland, Colo.: Alpine Publications, 1994.

Kowalski, Gary. *Goodbye, Friend: Healing Wisdom for Anyone Who Has Ever Lost a Pet.* Walpole, N.H.: Stillpoint Publishing, 1997.

Milani, Myrna. *Preparing for the Loss of Your Pet: Saying Goodbye with Love, Dignity and Peace of Mind.* Rocklin, Calif.: Prima Publishing, 1998.

Reynolds, Rita M. *Blessing the Bridge: What Animals Teach Us about Death, Dying, and Beyond.* Troutdale, Ore: NewSage Press, 2001.

Sife, Wallace. *The Loss of a Pet.* New York: Howell Book House/Macmillan General Reference, 1998.

Other resources
http://www.pet-loss.net
Includes a state-by-state listing of pet-loss support groups.

DIET
Books

Lonsdale, Tom. *Raw Meaty Bones Promote Health.* South Windsor, N.S.W.: Revetco P/L, 2001.

Martin, Ann. *Foods Pets Die For: Shocking Facts about Pet Food.* Troutdale, Ore.: NewSage Press, 1997.

McKay, Pat. *Reigning Cats and Dogs,* rev. ed. Pasadena, Calif.: Oscar Publications, 1996.

Palika, Liz. *The Consumer's Guide to Cat Food.* New York: Howell Book House/ Macmillan General Reference, 1997.

Schultze, Kymythy. *Natural Nutrition for Dogs and Cats: The Ultimate Diet*. Carlsbad, Calif.: Hay House, 1998.

Strombeck, Donald. *Home-Prepared Dog and Cat Diets: The Healthful Alternative*. Ames, Iowa: Iowa State University Press, 1999.

Websites

For information on feeding raw food to cats:

RawCats yahoogroup
subscribe@RawCats@yahoogroups.com

Holisticat Web site and mailing list
www.holisticat.com

Sources for prepared raw-food diets

Aunt Jeni's Homemade 4 Life
P.O. Box 124
Temple Hills, Maryland 20757
301-702-0123
www.auntjeni.com

Bravo Raw Diet
c/o Manchester Packing Company, Inc.
349 Wetherell Street
Manchester, CT 06040-6349
860-693-0632
www.bravorawdiet.com

Nature's Variety
6200 North 56th Street
P.O. Box 29345
Lincoln, NE 68529-0345
888-519-7387
www.naturesvariety.com

Oma's Pride
Miller Foods, Inc.
308 Arch Road
Avon, CT 06001
800-678-6627
www.omaspride.com

Steve's Real Food
Eugene, OR
888-526-1900
www.stevesrealfood.com

Snake-food suppliers (for whole foods for cats)
Zoological Pet Food, Inc.
31 Southard Road
Stephentown, NY 12168
800-GET-RATS
www.miceonice.com

Rodent Pro.com
Evansville, IN
812-867-7598
www.rodentpro.com

FLOWER REMEDIES
Books
Ball, Stefan, and Judy Howard. *Bach Flower Remedies for Animals*. Essex, UK: The
    C. W. Daniel Company, 1999.

Callahan, Sharon. *Healing Animals Naturally with Flower Essences and Intuitive Listening*. Mt. Shasta, Calif.: Sacred Spirit Publishing, 2001.

Sources for flower remedies:
Bach flower remedies are available at most health food stores. Information on Bach
flower remedies can be found at *www.bachcentre.com*

Anaflora
P.O. Box 1056
Mt. Shasta, CA 96067
530-926-6424
Fax: 530-926-1245
www.anaflora.com

Flower Essence Services (FES)
P.O. Box 1769
Nevada City, CA 95959
800-548-0075
Fax: 530-265-6467
www.floweressence.com

Green Hope Farm
P.O. Box 125
Meriden, NH 03770
603-469-6332
Fax: 603-469-3790
www.greenhopeessences.com

A wide selection of flower essences, from various companies, is available at *www.essencesonline.com*.

HEALTH
Books

Ballner, Maryjean. *Cat Massage: A Whiskers-to-Tail Guide to Your Cat's Ultimate Petting Experience*. New York: St. Martin's Press, 1997.

Fogle, Bruce. *Natural Cat Care: Fresh Approaches to Caring for Your Cat from the World's Best-Selling Practicing Vet*. New York: DK Publishing, 1999.

Goldstein, Martin. *The Nature of Animal Healing: The Definitive Holistic Medicine Guide for Caring for Your Dog and Cat*. New York: Ballantine Books, 2000.

Hamilton, Don. *Homeopathic Care for Dogs and Cats: Small Doses for Small Animals*. Berkeley, Calif.: North Atlantic Books, 1999.

Kelleher, Donna. *The Last Chance Dog: And Other True Stories of Holistic Animal Healing*. New York: Scribner, 2003.

Lazarus, Pat. *Keep Your Cat Healthy the Natural Way*. New York: Fawcett, 1999.

Messonier, DVM, Shawn. *Natural Health Bible for Dogs & Cats*. Roseville, Calif.: Prima Publishing, 2001.

Pitcairn, Richard, and Susan Hubble Pitcairn. *Dr. Pitcairn's Complete Guide to Natural Health for Dogs and Cats*, rev. ed. Emmaus, Penn.: Rodale, 1995.

Poynter, Dan. *The Older Cat: Recognizing Decline and Extending Life.* Santa Barbara: Para Publishing, 2001.

Puotinen, C. J. *The Encyclopedia of Natural Pet Care.* New Canaan, Conn.: Keats Publishing, 1998.

Puotinen, C. J. *Natural Remedies for Dogs and Cats.* Lincolnwood, Ill.: Keats Publishing, 1999.

Schwartz, Cheryl. *Four Paws, Five Directions: A Guide to Chinese Medicine for Cats and Dogs.* Berkeley, Calif.: Celestial Arts Publishing, 1996.

Schwartz, Cheryl. *Natural Healing for Dogs and Cats A–Z.* Carlsbad, Calif.: Hay House, 2000.

Shojai, Amy D. *The First Aid Companion for Dogs and Cats.* Emmaus, Penn.: Rodale Press, 2001.

Shojai, Amy D. *Pet Care in the New Century: Cutting Edge Medicine for Dogs and Cats.* New York: New American Library, 2001.

Wulff-Tilford, Mary L., and Gregory L. Tilford. *All You Ever Wanted to Know About Herbs for Pets.* Irvine, Calif.: Bowtie Press, 1999.

Zucker, Martin. *The Veterinarians' Guide to Natural Remedies for Cats: Safe and Effective Alternative Treatments and Healing Techniques from the Nations Top Holistic Veterinarians.* New York: Three Rivers Press, 1999.

Videos

Your Cat Wants a Massage! Maryjean Ballner, 1999.

First Aid Pet Emergency: Cats, Apogee Communication, 1998.

Websites

Vaccine-Associated Feline Sarcoma Task Force
www.avma.org/vafstf/default.asp

American Association of Feline Practitioners
www.aafponline.org

Holistic veterinary care Websites:
www.alvetmed.com: For information on alternative treatments for a variety of ailments, as well as directories of holistic practitioners.

www.listservice.net/wellpet/index.htm: The website of the long-running wellpet e-mail list provides abundant articles on a variety of pet-related alternative healing topics, many of them gleaned from the lists archives.

To find an animal hospital accredited by the American Animal Hospital Association: *www.healthypet.com*

Other resources
Pet Temp ear thermometer:
Advanced Monitors Corporation
6255 Ferris Square
San Diego, CA 92121 USA
877-738-8367
www.pet-temp.com

Nutritional supplements for arthritis
Cosequin for Cats
Nutramax Laboratories, Inc.
2208 Lakeside Boulevard,
Edgewood, MD 21040
800-925-5187

Glyco-Flex for Cats
Vetri-Science
800-882-9993
http://vetriscience.com/glycoflex1cats.html

Both of the above supplements are available through veterinarians or on-line at *www.healthypets.com.*

SeaFlex
Coast Side Bio Resources
P.O. Box 151
Stonington, ME 04681
800-732-8072
http://www.seacucumber.com/animals.html

Pet ramps and steps
HandiRamp
510 North Avenue
Libertyville, IL 60048
800-876-7267
http://www.handiramp.com/pet-ramp.htm

Discount Ramps.com
2410 South Main Street, Suite C
West Bend, WI 53095
888-651-3431
http://www.discountramps.com/half_step_pet_ramp.htm

Pet steps
C&D Pet Products
405 East D Street
Petaluma, CA 94952
888-554-7387
www.cdpets.com/steps.html

INDOOR/OUTDOOR SAFETY
Video catnip and a wide variety of toys
www.cattoys.com

Habikat cat window enclosure
Impress Your Pet
220 West 24th Street, 1H
New York, NY 10011
888-904-8425
www.habikat.com

Toxic and nontoxic plants
ASPCA Animal Poison Control Center:
www.apcc.aspca.org

Cat Fanciers' Association:
List of plants toxic to cats: *www.cfainc.org/articles/plants.html*
List of nontoxic plants: *www.cfainc.org/articles/plants-non-toxic.html*

Cat walking jacket
HDW Enterprises, Inc.
P.O. Box 418104
Sacramento, CA 95841-8104
916-481-2287
www.hdw-inc.com/walkingjackets.htm

Cat fences
Cat Fence-In
P.O. Box 795, Dept. E
Sparks, NV 89432
888-738-9099
www.catfencein.com

Affordable Cat Fence
722 West Kings Highway
San Antonio, TX, 78212
888-840-2287
www.catfence.com

Do-it-yourself cat fencing instructions/kits
Free instructions available on-line at *www.corporatevideo.com/klips/index.htm*

Information on a do-it-yourself cat fence kit, or to make cat fencing from materials available at a hardware store, is available from Alley Cat Allies, an organization dedicated to helping feral cats: *www.alleycat.org/pdf/fence.pdf*

Outdoor enclosures
C&D Pet Products
405 East D Street
Petaluma, CA 94952
888-554-7387
www.cdpets.com

CD&E Enterprises
800-528-2243
www.cde-animalcages.com

Kittywalk and Pet Stroller
Midnight Pass Inc.
149 Old Main Street, Suite 489
Marshfield Hills, MA 02051-0489
877-844-4438
www.midnightpass.com

Tree guards
Cat Fence-In
P.O. Box 795, Dept. E
Sparks, NV 89432
888-738-9099
www.catfencein.com

Litters and litter boxes
Litters
About.com discussions of litters: http://cats.about.com/cs/litterbox/

Problems with clumping litters: *http://www.thelighthouse-online.com/marina/articles/clump.html*

High-tech litter boxes
KittySuite
P.O. Box 940094
Maitland, FL 32794-0094
866-548-8978
www.kittysuite.com

LitterFree
Pet-Centric, Inc.
5677 Oberlin Drive, Suite 110
San Diego, CA 92121
858-550-2000
www.litterfree.com

Littermaid
Applica Consumer Products
6 Armstrong Road
Shelton, CT 06484
800-548-6243
www.littermaid.com

Litter Robot
Automated Pet Care Products, Inc.
40 West Howard, Suite B-5
Pontiac, MI 48342
877-250-7729
http://www.litter-robot.com

Litter disposal system
LitterLocker
Petmate
P.O. Box 1246
Arlington, TX 76004-1246
1877-PETMATE (877-738-6283)
www.petmate.com

Lost and found pets
Websites
www.1888pets911.org
www.petheartline.com
www.awolpet.com
www.missingpet.net
www.lostandfound.com

PET SITTERS

To find a pet sitter in your area, contact one of these associations:

National Association of Professional Pet Sitters
17000 Commerce Parkway, Suite C
Mt. Laurel, NJ 08054
800-296-PETS
Fax: 856-439-0525
www.petsitters.org

Pet Sitters International
201 East King Street
King, NC 27021-9161
336-983-9222
Fax: 336-983-5266
www.petsit.com

TELEPATHIC ANIMAL COMMUNICATION

Books

Adams, Janine. *You Can Talk to Your Animals: Animal Communicators Tell You How.* Foster City, Calif.: Howell Book House/IDG Books Worldwide, 2000.

Curtis, Anita. *Animal Wisdom: How to Hear the Animals.* New York: iUniverse, 2001.

Fitzpatrick, Sonya, with Patricia Burkhart Smith. *What the Animals Tell Me: Understanding Your Pet's Complex Emotions.* New York: Hyperion, 1997.

Gurney, Carol. *The Language of Animals: Seven Steps to Communicating with Animals.* New York: Dell, 2001.

Hiby, Lydia, with Bonnie S. Weintraub. *Conversations with Animals: Cherished Messages and Memories as Told by an Animal Communicator.* Troutdale, Ore.: NewSage Press, 1998.

Smith, Penelope. *Animal Talk: Interspecies Telepathic Communication,* 2nd ed. Hillsboro, Ore: Beyond Words Publishing, 1999.

Smith, Penelope. *When Animals Speak: Advanced Interspecies Communication,* 2nd ed. Hillsboro, Ore: Beyond Words Publishing, 1999.

Summers, Patty. *Talking with the Animals.* Charlottesville, Va.: Hampton Roads Publishing Company, 1998.

Websites
To find an animal communicator go to Penelope Smith's Web site: *www.animaltalk.net*

TRAVEL RESOURCES
Books
American Automobile Association. *Traveling with Your Pet: The AAA PetBook.* Orlando, FL: AAA, 2001. (AAA's regular TourBooks also indicate whether hotels accept pets.)

Arden, Andrea. *Fodor's Road Guide USA: Where to Stay with Your Pet.* New York: Fodor's Travel Publications, 2001.

Barish, Eileen. *Vacationing with Your Pet: Eileen's Directory of Pet-Friendly Lodging in the United States and Canada. Fifth Ed.* Scottsdale, AZ: Pet Friendly Publications, 2001.

Grayson, Fred, et al. *The Portable Pets Welcome.Com: The Complete Guide to Traveling with Your Pet.* New York: Howell Book House/Hungry Minds, 2001.

Carriers
SturdiProducts, makers of the SturdiBag carrier, as well as a portable litter pan and pet tent:
16751 East State Route 106
Belfair, WA 98528 USA
800-779-8193
www.sturdiproducts.com

Sherpa's Pet Trading Company, makers of the Sherpa Bag:
Gayle Martz, Inc.
135 East 55th Street
New York, NY 10022
212-838-9837
www.sherpapet.com

Doskocil/Petmate, makers of the Vari-Kennel (hard-sided plastic carrier):
P.O. Box 1246
Arlington, Texas 76004-1246
877-738-6283
www.petmate.com

Jiffy Tags (sturdy, temporary tags you can write on) are available from:
Animal Care Equipment & Services, Inc.
P.O. Box 3275
Crestline, CA 92325
800-338-ACES
www.animal-care.com

TELLINGTON TTOUCH
Book
Tellington-Jones, Linda and Sybil Taylor. *The Tellington TTouch: A Revolutionary Natural Method to Train and Care for Your Favorite Animal.* New York: Penguin Books, 1992.

Videos
The Tellington TTouch for Happier, Healthier Cats, Linda Tellington-Jones, 1992.

TTouch of Magic Video for Cats and Kittens, Linda Tellington-Jones, 1999.

Web site
To learn more about TTouch, see a schedule of seminars, or find a practitioner near you, go to founder Linda Tellington-Jones's Web site at: *www.tellingtontouch.com*

THE VACCINE CONTROVERSY
Books
Diodati, Catherine. *Vaccine Guide for Dogs and Cats: What Every Pet Owner Should Know.* Santa Fe NM: New Atlantean Press, 2003.

McKay, Pat. *Natural Immunity: Why You Should Not Vaccinate.* Pasadena, Calif.: Oscar Publications, 1997.

O'Driscoll, Catherine. *What Vets Don't Tell You About Vaccines.* Derbyshire, UK: Abbeywood Publishing, 2nd ed., 1998.

Index

Page numbers in **bold** indicate tables.

fat in, 120
feline lower urinary tract disease (fLUTD) and, 95, 134
fiber in, 109
finicky eating, 30, 190–92
free-feeding, 90, 91, 117, 118, 192
grains in, 93
home-prepared diet, 5, 94, 95–96, 191
illness from, 30, 93, 191, 192
label reading, 93
"lite" foods, 118
location for feeding, 89, 90–91, 188
meat in, 90, 93, 95, 112, 191
moving with your cat, 60
natural diet, 5, 89, 197
nutritional supplements, 28, 133, 231
obesity and, 31, 70, 90, 91, 112, 115–18
oils (essential fatty acids) in, 110, 120–21
preservatives caution, 93, 95, 112
privacy for feeding, 90
quality food, 5, 13, 90, 93, 95, 117, 121, 181
regular feedings, 90, 117
resources for, 226–28
tuna, 95
variety in, 93, 94, 190, 191, 192
water importance, 28–29, 95, 132
whole foods, 94
See also Treats
Digestive enzyme, 94
Dog food for cats, 96
Dogs and cats, 18, 44–47
Dogs vs. cats communication, xi, xii, xvi, 159, 161
Domestic vs. wildcats, xi–xii
Drapery cord safety, 76
Dried meats, 113
Drinkwell, 28
Dry foods, 95, 117, 134

Ears, body language, xiv–xv
Ear TTouch, xxiii, 27, 80, 124
Eating importance, 30, 60, 91, 118, 192. *See also* Diet
Electrical cord safety, 74–75
Emergencies, 123, 124
Enzymatic cleaner for urine, 204, 211–12
Equipment for cats, 12–15
Essence of Nature (flower essence), 144, 153
Essential fatty acids (oils) in diet, 110, 120–21
Euthanasia, 31, 97–99, 226
Excessive grooming, 179–81
Excessive meowing, xvi, 182–85
Eyes, body language, xiv–xv
Eyes (human) for communication, xviii–xix

Facial pheromones, xiii, xv, xvii–xviii, xxii. *See also* Feliway
    products
Fasting, 91, 118, 192
Fat in diet, 120
Fatty liver disease (hepatic lipidosis), 30, 60, 91, 118, 192
Fauna Communication Research Institute, xvii
Fearful aggressive body language, **xv**
Fearful cats, **xiv**, 167

Feline communication, xi–xxv
    body language (cats), xiii, **xiv–xv**, xvi, 160, 167, 168
    body language (human), xviii–xix
    dogs vs., xi, xii, xvi, 159, 161
    domestic vs. wildcats, xi–xii
    eyes (human) for, xviii–xix
    management (manipulating situation) for, xxiv
    origins of, xi–xiii
    pheromones for, xiii–xv, xxii
    predators and cat behavior, xii
    purring, xvii
    resources for, 223–37
    solitary creatures, xii
    telepathic communication, xix–xx, 235–36
    touch, xvii xviii
    vocalizations, xvi–xvii
    voice (human) for, xix, xviii
    See also Behavior challenges; Care of your cat; Feliway
        products; Flower essences (remedies); Health and safety;
        Indoor/outdoor issues; Play (interactive); Tellington
        TTouch; Territoriality of cats; Training cats
Feline lower urinary tract disease (fLUTD), 28, 60, 95,
    131–34
Feliway products
    babies and children, 8
    bringing new cat home, 17
    carriers for cats, 34
    clawing furniture, 176
    counter walking, 226
    facial pheromone (synthetic), xxii
    fighting with other cats, 188
    indoor/outdoor issues, 145
    moving with your cat, 59
    spraying (urine marking), 212
    traveling with your cat, 80
    veterinarian visits, 106
Fencing yards, 156
Fiber in diet, 109
Fighting with other cats, 186–89
Filters for allergies, 4
Finding lost cats, 48–51, 235
Finicky eating, 30, 190–92
First Aid Companion for Dogs and Cats, The (Shojai), 124
Fleas, 180
Flour to stop bleeding quicks, 64
Flower Essence Services, xxiv
Flower essences (remedies), xxiii–xxiv
    brushing/combing cats, 24
    dogs and cats, 46
    grooming (excessive), 180
    indoor/outdoor issues, 144, 153
    moving with your cat, 59
    resources for, 228–29
    shyness, 208
    spraying (urine marking), 212
fLUTD (feline lower urinary tract disease), 28, 60, 95, 131–34
Flying with cats, 81
Food. *See* Diet
Forcing cats on others, 82
Frazier, Anitra, 22, 24, 86, 91, 192, 204

Free-feeding, 90, 91, 117, 118, 192
Friendly body language, **xiv**
Furniture, clawing, 174–78

Geriatric (aging) cats, 26–31
Getting Started: Clicker Training for Cats (Pryor), xxi, 40, 41, 222
Glycoflex for Cats, 28
Good Dog! (flower essence), 46
Grains in diet, 93
Grass for cats, 194
Green Hope Farm, xxiv, 180
Greeting cats, spots for, 154, 172, 173
Grieving, 99, 226
Grooming cats. *See* Brushing/combing cats
Grooming (excessive), 179–81

Habikat, 153
Hairballs, 14, 23, 108–10
Hair coat, body language, **xiv–xv,** 5
Halo Dinner Party, 192
Hanging plants, 194
Happiness indoors, 151–54
Harmony (flower essence), 46
Harnesses for cats, 159–60, 173
Hart, B. L., 211
Head butt, xiv
Healing and purring, xvii
Health and safety, 83–139
    euthanasia, 31, 97–99, 226
    hairballs, 14, 23, 108–10
    medications, giving, 100–103
    resources for, 229–33
    shedding, 119–21
    spaying and neutering, xiv–xv, 127–30, 150, 184, 211
    treats, 37, 42, 111–14, 117
    urinary tract problems, 28, 60, 95, 131–34
    vaccinations, 30, 135–39, 237
    veterinarian visits, 104–7
    See also Csre of your cat; Declawing; Diet; Illness in cats; Indoor/Outdoor issues
Healthy Coat (flower essence), 180
Heartland Wheat Litter, 53, 54
Hepatic lipidosis (fatty liver disease), 30, 60, 91, 118, 192
Hiding, cats' love of, 49, 50, 153, 208
High-tech litter boxes, 54–55
Holistic veterinarians, 133, 135, 230–31
Home-prepared diet, 5, 94, 95–96, 191
Housecat: How to Keep Your Indoor Cat Sane and Sound (Church), 148
Houseplant eating, 74, 193–96
Humane Society (U. S.), 87
Hunting, xii, xiii, xx–xxi, 151, 152, 197–99

Identification tags for cats, 14–15, 49, 58, 75, 79, 81
Illness in cats
    after-hours veterinary clinic, 124
    aging (geriatric) cats, 27, 28, 30, 31
    biting/scratching and, 165, 166

cancer, 30
constipation, 28
cystitis (bladder inflammation), 131
diabetes, 28, 29
diarrhea, 79
diet and, 30, 93, 191, 192
Ear TTouch for, xxiii, 27, 80, 124
emergencies, 123, 124
fatty liver disease (hepatic lipidosis), 30, 60, 91, 118, 192
feline lower urinary tract disease (fLUTD), 28, 60, 95, 131–34
finicky eating and, 30, 191, 192
grooming (excessive) and, 179
inner voice, listening to your, 125
kidney disease, 28, 29, 135
listening to cats, 125
litter box use and, 123, 132, 134, 202, 203
lymphoma, 76–77
meowing and, 183
moving with your cat and, 60
poisonous plants, 74, 194, 195–96
renal failure, 30
shedding (excessive) and, 120, 121
shyness and, 208, 209
signs of, 122–26
temperature, taking, 124–25
upper respiratory diseases, 60
urinary tract problems, 28, 60, 95, 131–34
vitamin-E deficiency, 95
weight changes and, 30, 116, 124
yellow fat disease (steatitis), 95
See also Health and safety; Veterinarians
Incisions, monitoring, 128–29
Indoor/outdoor issues, 141–61
    aging (geriatric) cats, 27
    declawed cats, 87, 150, 157
    happiness indoors, 151–54
    indoor cat, decisions about, 143, 147–50
    leash-training cats, 82, 155–56, 158–61
    moving with your cat and, 60
    outdoor cat, converting into indoor cat, 143–46
    outdoor experiences (safe), 145, 154, 155–57, 172
    quantity vs. quality-of-life, 132, 148
    resources for, 232–33
    risks for outdoor cats, 141, 148–49
    safety issues, 74, 141–42, 148, 155
    vaccinations, 136
Inner voice, listening to your, 125
Instructions (written) for pet sitters, 68
Interactive play. *See* Play (interactive)
Internet
    for lost cats, 50, 235
    for resources, 226, 227, 230–31, 236, 237
Introducing cats to other pets, 18–19

Jeffries, Wendy, 42
Jiffy Tag, 79
Johnson-Bennett, Pam, xvi, 72, 154, 172, 188